G. Ferstl
846-0279

The Pocket Dictionary of
LEGAL WORDS

The Pocket Dictionary of
LEGAL WORDS

JOHN J. KASAIAN

Edited by DOUGLAS B. OLIVER, J.D.

A DOLPHIN BOOK

Doubleday & Company, Inc.
Garden City, New York
1979

Library of Congress Cataloging in Publication Data

Kasaian, John J
The pocket dictionary of legal words.

"A Dolphin book."
1. Law—United States—Dictionaries. I. Oliver, Douglas B. II. Title.
KF156.K24 340'.03
ISBN: 0-385-14840-2
Library of Congress Catalog Card Number 78-20237

Printed in the United States of America
First Edition

To my parents,
John and Dorothy

Preface

This dictionary is meant to be used as a handy reference for people who, in the course of their business, education, or other activities, are exposed to the complex and often bewildering vocabulary of the lawyer.

The entries have been carefully selected to encompass the most common and potentially confusing words and terms the average person is likely to find in the areas of criminal, tort, business, environmental, and tax law; real estate; finance; procedure; and estates. Definitions are designed to provide clear, understandable explanations of the terms used in the legal world.

This is by no means a definitive work and should not be used in place of such standard reference books as Black's Law Dictionary or Bouvier's. Our goal has been to provide a basic knowledge of legal language that will enable you to understand what your lawyer—or theirs—is talking about.

If you cannot find the term you want, keep in mind that many words are actually variations on a common root and not all the variations may be printed as separate entries. In order to find the term you want, try scanning the pages while looking for other words sharing the same root. If that fails, used the table of prefixes and suffixes (Appendix B) and try to reconstruct the term you need and its meaning.

NOTE: Unless otherwise indicated, *italicized* entries are in Latin.

J.J.K.

Acknowledgments

I am very grateful for the help, enthusiasm, and support of Dr. Kenneth Seib, of the California State University, Fresno. I wish to thank my mother, who took on the task of typing the entire manuscript. I also wish to thank the many scholars and researchers whose hornbooks, treatises, lexicons, and dictionaries have provided the foundation on which our understanding of the law rests.

Contents

◀ A ▶

A.B.A. The abbreviation for the American Bar Association.

ABACTION Cattle stealing.

ABANDONMENT 1. The desertion of a spouse. 2. Grounds for a divorce for deserting a spouse. 3. The voluntary surrendering of right to real or personal property, without passing the rights to someone else. 4. The giving up of something as a total loss.

ABATEMENT 1. A reduction or termination (of something). 2. The overthrowing or quashing of a lawsuit because of some technicality, without barring the plaintiff from recommencing the lawsuit.

ABDUCTION Kidnaping.

ABEYANCE The condition of something, especially an estate, whose lawful owner has not been found.

Ab initio From the beginning.

ABJURATION A sworn denial, renunciation, or abandonment.

ABJURATION OF ALLEGIANCE An oath taken by naturalized citizens renouncing loyalty owed to any foreign government.

ABJURE To take an oath of denial, renunciation, or abandonment.

ABORTION The miscarriage or premature expulsion of a fetus. Abortions can be either spontaneous (taking place unexpectedly) or induced (intentionally caused). An abortion is said to be therapeutic when the miscarriage is induced for medical reasons. Induced abortions are illegal when performed contrary to the law.

ABROGATE To pass a law which repeals or annuls.

ABSCOND 1. To hide oneself in order to avoid judicial process. 2. To flee or depart suddenly to avoid judicial process.

ABSOLUTE Complete, entire, or unconditional.

Absque hoc Without this.

ABSTENTION A doctrine permitting a federal court to decline to try a case, leaving it to be decided instead by a state court.

ABSTRACT 1. (n.) The essence or a summary (of something). 2. (v). To withdraw or take away from.

ABSTRACT OF TITLE A brief history of the ownership of a piece of real property.

ABUSE OF PROCESS The crime of misusing civil or criminal process in order to achieve an unlawful goal or to annoy someone, as when a creditor obtains a warrant for the arrest of a debtor in order to coerce the debtor into paying what he owes.

ABUSE, SEXUAL 1. An injury to the genital organs, occurring during an attempt at intercourse. 2. Injury to a child's genital organs, especially those of a female, short of penetration.

ABUT Be next to or in physical contact with (something else).

ABUTTER The owner of property that borders or abuts property owned by another.

ACCELERATION CLAUSE A clause that makes a debt become immediately due should the debtor fail to perform some specified obligation.

ACCEPTANCE 1. The act of assenting to an offer to make a contract. 2. The act of receiving something. 3. The act of agreeing to something.

ACCESS The right or means of approaching, the ability to approach; especially a husband's ability to have sexual relations with his wife, or the ability of customers to approach a place of business from the street.

ACCESSION A right to something that has become a part of something already owned. For an example, if a tree grows on a piece of property, the landowner then owns the tree as well as the property.

ACCESSORY A person who aids in the commission of a crime (though not actually present at the time the crime is committed) by knowingly giving aid to a criminal.

ACCESSORY AFTER THE FACT A person who conceals or aids someone he knows has committed a crime, thus enabling the criminal to escape punishment.

ACCESSORY BEFORE THE FACT A person who counsels or encourages another in the commission of a crime but who is not present at the incident.

ACCIDENT An unexpected, unplanned event usually involving some loss or injury.

ACCOMMODATION PAPER A note from a third party written for the purpose of recommending a person for a loan.

ACCOMPLICE A person who knowingly and voluntarily aids another in the attempt to commit, or the commission of, a crime. Presence at the scene of the crime is not necessary.

ACCORD AND SATISFACTION A debtor's payment in money or property, sometimes worth less than the debt owed, upon receipt of which the debtee agrees to extinguish the debt.

ACCOUNT A written record or statement of money received and paid out.

ACCOUNTS RECEIVABLE A record of money owed to a person or business and not yet received.

ACCOUNT STATED A figure representing exactly what is owed, as calculated by the person to whom the debt is owed.

ACCRUAL The accumulation or gathering (of something, particularly something of value such as property or interest on money in a savings account).

ACCRUED (Profits or benefits) due and payable from an investment.

ACCUSATION A formal charge, made in court, that a person is guilty of a crime.

ACCUSED 1. A person who is charged with having committed a crime. 2. The defendant in a criminal trial.

ACKNOWLEDGMENT The admission or acceptance of something as genuine, especially of a document as the act of the person signing it.

ACKNOWLEDGMENT OF PATERNITY A man's declaration that he is the father of a child.

ACQUIESCENCE The conduct from which consent or guilt may be implied; passive compliance.

ACQUISITION The gaining of ownership of property.

ACQUIT To release or set free from some burden or obligation, especially from a criminal accusation made in court.

ACQUITTAL A judge or jury's release from prosecution of a person accused of a crime. An acquittal acts as a certification of innocence.

ACT 1. A term for certain types of laws passed by Congress or the state legislators. 2. That which is done.

ACT OF GOD An event occurring by the violence of nature, without any human interference. An event of an unpredictable nature. Example: an earthquake.

Actio criminalis A criminal action.

Actio damni injuria A lawsuit for damages.

Actio ex delicto A court action arising out of a tort.

ACTION 1. A court proceeding whereby one party charges another with the infringement of his rights or seeks to prevent another from infringing on his rights. 2. A person's behavior.

ACTIONABLE Providing grounds for a lawsuit.

ACTUAL CASH VALUE The fair cash price for property during the normal course of business.

ACTUARY An officer of an insurance company charged with computing values and statistics.

Actus reus A criminal act.

Ad hoc For this; for a specific purpose.

Ad infinitum To an infinite extent; something that is unlimited.

Ad litem For a particular lawsuit.

ADDICT A person who has a habit he is unable to control, especially the habitual taking of drugs.

Additur It is increased. Usually refers to a court's award of damages exceeding the amount asked for by the plaintiff or awarded by a jury.

ADEMPTION A person's gift or disposition, while alive, of something already mentioned in his will making it impossible to carry out the will after his death.

ADEQUATE Suitable; sufficient.

ADHESION CONTRACT A one-sided contract resulting from an unequal bargaining situation. For example, if a buyer has no choice but to buy from a particular seller, the buyer is forced to pay whatever the seller asks.

ADJECTIVE LAWS Laws that govern the procedures by which courts operate.

ADJOURN To postpone or put off until a later time. For example, a court might adjourn for the day and continue with the trial the next morning.

ADJUDICATE To proceed to a final decision on a case. By a judge.

ADJUDICATION The pronouncing or recording of a judgment at the conclusion of a trial.

ADMINISTRATION 1. The management of the estate of a decedent, until the estate can be settled by satisfying debts and distributing property. 2. The management of the country's affairs by the President. 3. The management of an organization.

ADMINISTRATIVE LAW An area of the law dealing with the management of government agencies.

ADMINISTRATOR, ADMINISTRATRIX (FEM.) A person authorized by the court to manage an estate.

ADMIRALTY LAW The civil and criminal law relating to occurrences on the high seas.

ADMISSIBLE EVIDENCE Information that is allowed and

proper to be used in reaching a decision in a judicial proceeding.

ADMISSION To admit to something; a confession.

ADOPTION 1. The act of becoming a foster parent to a child born of another person and accepting the rights and duties arising from parenthood. 2. The passage of a bill into law. 3. The acceptance of something as one's own.

ADULTERY The act of voluntary sexual intercourse between one person and another person's spouse.

ADVERSARY An opponent, especially in court.

ADVERSE POSSESSION The occupancy or enjoyment of property in spite of, and in defiance of, someone else's legal title. If such possession continues for twenty years, legal title can be claimed by the one in possession. Adverse possession must be actual possession, continuous, visible, and hostile to the one who has legal title.

ADVERTISEMENT A notice, the purpose of which is to inform the general public.

ADVICE 1. Knowledge of a professional or technical nature that is given to a client. 2. An opinion or viewpoint.

ADVOCATE To support, defend, or publicly speak in favor of.

AFFIANT A person who takes an oath swearing to tell the truth in an affidavit.

AFFIDAVIT A written statement witnessed by an authorized officer of the court and made under oath.

AFFILIATE 1. (n.) Something allied, connected, or united with a larger group. 2. (v.) To withdraw or take from.

AFFINITY The relationship arising, from the marriage, between a person and the blood relatives of his spouse.

AFFIRM To confirm, support, or approve, especially in a higher court's approval or support of a lower court's decision.

AFFIRMATIVE DEFENSE A defendant's answer, to a complaint by a plaintiff, that presents new arguments and facts instead of denying the facts put forward in the original complaint.

AFFIRMATIVE RELIEF A benefit or gain that is owed a defendant, independent of the plaintiff's original claim.

AFFRAY A fight or brawl in a public place.

A fortiori Resulting from stronger reasoning.

AGENCY A relationship between two parties in which one party is authorized by the other to act on his behalf.

AGENCY, GOVERNMENT A branch of the local, state, or federal government authorized to perform functions such as law enforcement or administration.

AGENT A person authorized to act on the behalf of another.

AGGRAVATION Those things or acts that increase the guilt for and consequences of an act. Aggravation usually increases the damages that can be awarded in a civil suit.

AGGRIEVED Having suffered from a loss or injury.

AGREEMENT 1. A contract. 2. A mutual understanding between two or more parties, not necessarily reduced to writing.

AID AND ABET To knowingly incite or help to commit (a crime).

AIR RIGHTS The right to use the space above a piece of real property.

ALEATORY CONTRACT A contract that depends on an uncertain event happening to one of the parties to the contract.

ALIAS 1. Also known as. 2. An assumed identity.

ALIBI A factual account of a suspect's activities at the time a crime was committed, offered as proof of the suspect's innocence.

ALIEN A person who is not a citizen or subject of the country where he is living.

ALIENATION The lawful transfer of title and possession of real property from one party to another, in which the former owner gives up the rights he once had to the property.

ALIENATION OF AFFECTION 1. The breakup of a marriage by a third person. 2. The malicious, willful attempt to destroy a marital relationship between two people, often by disgracing or humiliating one spouse in front of the other.

ALIMONY The financial support paid to a divorced spouse, the sum of which is ordered by the court.

ALIMONY ANNUITY An income for life or for a duration of time, provided for a divorced spouse.

ALIMONY ARREARS Alimony payments that are behind.

ALIMONY *pendente lite* An allowance made pending a suit for divorce, usually including money for support as well as for maintaining the suit for divorce.

ALLEGE To make an allegation.

ALLEGATION A statement made by one party, who then attempts to prove it to be fact.

ALLOCUTION The opportunity a trial judge gives the prisoner to speak for himself and offer his reasons why he should escape sentencing.

ALTERATION The changing of something, but not to the extent of destroying it or starting something new.

AMANUENSIS A person who writes down what another person dictates; a person who takes dictation.

AMBIGUITY Something misleading or unclear, not definite or concrete; that which is without specific meaning, so that it may be interpreted in several ways.

AMBULATORY AUTOMATISM A condition of a person who unconsciously wanders around doing things he would not normally do and is therefore not responsible for.

AMBUSH 1. A surprise attack from a hiding place. 2. The hiding place where attackers lie in wait. 3. To lie in wait for.

AMENDMENT 1. An additional provision to the Constitution. 2. A change in a bill or law.

AMENDMENT TO PLEADING A correction or change made in a written statement of the facts as submitted by the opposing sides to a lawsuit.

AMENITY Something about or added to a piece of real property which makes it more desirable than other pieces of land; for example, a scenic view or improvements such as landscaping.

Amentia Insanity; idiocy.

Amicus curiae 1. A friend of the court, a bystander who volunteers needed information to the court. 2. A bystander not a party to a lawsuit who is allowed to present an argument or evidence in court in order to protect his own interests.

AMNESIA Loss of memory.

AMNESTY 1. Forgiveness. 2. Freedom from prosecution for some crime.

AMORTIZATION The payment of a debt through regular, uniform payments.

Animo cancellandi With intention to void, or cancel.

Animus capiendi With intention to take, seize, or capture.

Animus derelinquendi Intent to abandon, or desert.

Animus differendi Intent to delay.

Animus furandi With felonious intent to steal.

Animus testandi With intent to make a will.

ANNEX To add to, attach.

ANNUAL PERCENTAGE RATE The yearly cost of a loan or a purchase made on time, based on a percentage of the balance of money owed.

ANNUITANT A person who receives an annuity.

ANNUITY An income for a period of years or for life.

ANNUL To void.

ANNULMENT 1. The act of voiding something, such as an agreement. 2. The voiding of a marriage, thereby eliminating the legal history of the marriage being annulled, as opposed to divorce, which only dissolves a marriage.

ANSWER A response made to a complaint in a court proceeding.

Ante Before.

ANTENUPTIAL AGREEMENT A premarital agreement that somehow modifies or makes definite the property rights of the parties involved.

ANTICIPATORY BREACH A party's refusal to carry out a contract obligation, before the time the obligation is required to be performed.

ANTITRUST ACTS A name given several statutes, both state and federal, enacted to protect against monopolies and promote competition.

APHASIA Loss of the ability to speak.

APPARENT DEFECT A visible, obvious flaw (in goods).

APPEAL To go to a higher court in an attempt to correct the decision of a lower court.

APPEARANCE A showing up in court, either personally or through one's representative.

APPELLANT A person who appeals to a higher court to correct the decision of a lower court.

APPELLATE COURT A court that hears appeals.

APPELLEE The party against whom an appeal is made.

APPOINT To name (someone), to a post or as the recipient of property.

APPORTION To divide into separate portions.

APPORTIONMENT The division of rights and liabilities according to the interests of the parties concerned.

APPRAISE To estimate the worth of something.

APPRECIATION IN VALUE An increase in the worth of something, not including improvements made to it that also would increase the value. Examples would include a painting that becomes more valuable after the painter's death or an antique, which becomes more valuable as it gets older.

APPREHENSION 1. The capture of a criminal suspect. 2. Fear.

APPURTENANCE A part of or an addition to something.

APT Suitable; appropriate.

AQUATIC RIGHTS The right to use bodies of water for fishing and navigation.

ARBITRAGE The buying of stocks or bills in one market and selling in another for a profit resulting from the difference of price between the two markets.

ARBITRARY Resulting from one's opinion or will; not according to a fixed standard.

ARBITRATION The taking of a dispute to an unbiased third party, usually named by the disputing parties, whose decision is binding.

ARBITRATION CLAUSE A clause in a contract stating that in the event of a dispute the parties agree to be bound by the decision of an arbitrator.

ARBITRATOR A person who arbitrates; an unbiased third party brought in to settle some dispute.

Arma in armatos sumere jura sinunt The law permits the use of arms against armed persons.

Arma moluta Sharp weapons used for cutting: knives, swords, and edged daggers.

ARMORY A building where weapons and supplies of ammunition are stored.

ARRAIGNMENT A judicial proceeding in which the defendant hears the charges brought against him and enters his plea.

ARREST 1. To detain (a person suspected of committing a crime). 2. To stop or put a halt to.

ARRESTEE A person who has been placed under arrest.

ARRESTOR 1. A person who arrests someone. 2. A person who brings a lawsuit against a debtor to take property in payment.

ARREST OF JUDGMENT The holding up of a judgment because of a defect in the proceedings.

ARREST UNDER WARRANT The arrest (of a person) made under the authority of a warrant.

ARREST WITHOUT WARRANT The arrest (of a person) not made under the authority of a warrant.

ARSON The crime of maliciously setting fire to a building or property. Some states divide arson into various categories, or degrees: First-degree arson usually consists of setting fire to a home. Lesser degrees include, depending on state law, setting fire to a building other than a house but dangerously close to one, and setting fire to any building other than a dwelling.

ASPORTATION The carrying away of the property of another.

ASSAULT The intentional and unlawful causing of apprehension of immediate bodily harm to another.

ASSAY The testing of metals, especially metallic ore and gold.

ASSERT To state or declare (something) as being the truth.

ASSESSMENT 1. A method of determining the contributions of several people toward a common objective according to the benefit received by each contributor, especially for taxation purposes. 2. A move by the Internal Revenue Service against a taxpayer for taxes owed to the government. 3. The fixing of a value for some property, or the amount of damages.

ASSETS Everything that can be used to pay creditors. Often used to mean all the property of a dead person.

ASSETS OF THE ESTATE IN BANKRUPTCY Property belonging to the bankrupt party, which can be used to help pay off the creditors.

ASSIGN 1. To formally transfer something to another person or party. 2. To appoint to a particular duty or responsibility.

ASSIGNMENT FOR BENEFIT OF CREDITORS The transfer in trust of property from a debtor to an assignee, who then pays off the debts. This is usually regulated by state statutes.

ASSUMPSIT A type of lawsuit in which one party seeks to enforce a broken promise that has caused him to suffer a loss of some kind.

ASSUMPTION OF RISK The act of knowingly and voluntarily doing something hazardous.

AT ARM'S LENGTH Beyond the reach or control of a particular party.

AT BAR Having the attention of the court.

AT LARGE Not bound or limited to any particular place or matter; free to roam.

ATTACHMENT The lawful seizure (of property) by the court during a lawsuit in order to secure the property until the controversy is resolved, so that the plaintiff can have recourse against it. If the defendant lives outside the state or the territory where the court has jurisdiction, his property within the jurisdiction of the court will be seized, and if he does not appear in court, the court gives the authority to dispose of the property to the plaintiff.

ATTEMPT An intent to do something, coupled with an act that falls short of the desired end.

ATTESTATION Evidence, provided by a witness, that a written instrument has been executed.

ATTESTING WITNESS A witness who attests that a written instrument has been executed.

ATTORNEY 1. A person hired to represent a client in matters dealing with the law. 2. A person hired to act in the place of another.

ATTORNEY GENERAL The chief legal adviser and representative for the federal government (appointed by the President). State governments have their own attorney generals to advise and represent their respective states.

ATTORNEY AT LAW An attorney who prepares and tries cases in court.

ATTORNEY IN FACT An attorney who is authorized by a client to manage either a particular matter or a business deal on the client's behalf.

ATTRACTIVE NUISANCE A dangerous piece of property that attracts trespassers unable to perceive the danger. Example:

a deep pit with slick sides that might cause a child to fall into it.

AUCTION A public sale of real or personal property, goods, rights, or livestock to the highest bidder.

AUCTIONEER A person licensed to conduct an auction.

AUDIT 1. An examination or study. 2. An examination (of an account) in order to certify that the bookkeeping records are accurate. 3. The procedure for examining bookkeeping records.

AUDITOR An officer charged with examination of books or accounts and certifying the accuracy of the records.

AUTHORITY 1. A power or right given to a person by another. 2. A public body charged with specified powers within a jurisdiction.

AUTOMOBILE-ACCIDENT REPARATION The award of damages for injuries resulting from an automobile accident.

AUTOPSY The examination of a dead body in order to determine the cause of death.

AVERMENT A positive statement of facts presented to the court in opposition to arguments presented by the other side.

AVOIDABLE CONSEQUENCES Results that can be avoided.

AWARD To give, grant, or present (something to another) for a good reason.

◀ B ▶

BACK-SEAT DRIVER A passenger in an automobile who disturbs the driver with unnecessary warnings and criticism regarding the driver's control over the automobile.

BACK TAXES Unpaid taxes for the previous year or years.

BACK WAGES Earnings owed an employee for previous work.

BADGE OF FRAUD Something about a contract that creates a suspicion that the contract is fradulent.

BAIL A sum of money that a prisoner deposits with the court in order to gain release from jail while his case awaits trial. This is to ensure the defendant's presence in court at his trial.

BAILEE A person who is trusted with another person's property, to take care of the property as directed by the owner of the property. Example: a warehouseman.

BAILIFF A deputy sheriff or other peace officer whose duty is to keep the peace in the courtroom, guard prisoners, and give assistance to the judge and jurors when required.

BAILIWICK In modern terms, the geographical area where an officer of the court has authority.

BAILMENT The delivery of property from an owner (bailor) to someone who is to take care of it (bailee).

BAILOR A person who owns goods held by a bailee.

BAIT AND SWITCH To lure customers into a store by advertising a specific item on sale, then convincing the customers to buy a different, more expensive product. The advertised item is usually claimed to be out of stock.

BANK 1. A commercial firm in the business of safekeeping and investing money. 2. A full group of judges who decide a case together (also "banc").

BANKRUPT A person who is unable to pay his debts and is determined insolvent by a bankruptcy court.

BANKRUPTCY ADJUDICATION A formal judgment, made by a court, declaring a party to be bankrupt.

BANKRUPTCY PROCEEDINGS The performance of certain acts necessary to be adjudged bankrupt.

BANKRUPTCY TRUSTEE A person who is appointed by a court to take care of the property of a bankrupt party until it can be divided among the creditors.

BAR 1. The lawyers permitted to practice law in a particular state. 2. To prohibit or ban. 3. A business engaged in selling alcoholic beverages for consumption on the premises.

BARGAIN A voluntary agreement for the purchase, sale, or exchange of goods.

BARRATRY A crime consisting of the starting of a groundless lawsuit.

BARRISTER An English trial lawyer.

BARTER The exchange or trade of goods for goods, as opposed to purchasing goods with money.

BASIS 1. A foundation or support. 2. A reason or cause for something.

BASTARDY PROCEEDINGS The legal process of getting the father of an illegitimate child to pay money for the child's support.

BATF Abbreviation for the Bureau of Alcohol, Tobacco, and Firearms.

BATTERY An intentional, unconsented-to, and unlawful touching, beating, seizing, or physical injury of another person.

BAWDYHOUSE A house of prostitution; a brothel.

Bellum War.

BENCH 1. The seat in a courtroom where a judge sits. 2. The name given a group of judges permitted to hear cases in a particular jurisdiction.

BENCH WARRANT A warrant issued by a judge to the legal authorities for the arrest of a person.

BENEFICIARY A person who profits from an insurance policy or trust.

BEQUEATH To give one's possessions—strictly, one's personal property—(to another) by means of a will.

BEQUEST A gift by will—strictly, a gift by will of personal property.

BESTIALITY Sexual intercourse between a human and a lower animal.

BET A wager.

BIA The abbreviation for the Bureau of Indian Affairs.

BID An offer to buy something at a price set by the offerer, which the seller may accept or reject in favor of a higher bid.

BIGAMIST A man or woman who is married to more than one person at the same time.

BIGAMY The criminal offense of having more than one spouse.

BILL 1. A written statement, of certain facts found by a lower court, that is sent to a higher court scheduled to hear an appeal. 2. An amount of money, stated in writing, due someone who supplies something of value. 3. A proposal for new governmental legislation. 4. A statement of charges, against a person, that is presented to a grand jury. 5. An unconditional order to a bank or someone else to pay a specified sum of money to someone.

BILL OF EXCHANGE A written and signed order commanding a second party to pay a specified sum to a third party. Unlike a check, it need not be drawn on a deposit.

BILL OF INDICTMENT A formal document, presented to a grand jury, that accuses somebody of having committed a crime.

BILL OF LADING An acknowledgment, in writing, of the receipt of goods.

BILL OF PARTICULARS A detailed statement, of the crimes or other wrongs that a defendant is accused of having committed, that enables the defendant to be aware of the exact charges against him.

BILL OF RIGHTS 1. The first ten amendments to the United States Constitution. 2. A declaration of the rights and privileges afforded to citizens in state constitutions. 3. An English document that states the rights and privileges granted to the citizens of Great Britain.

BILL OF SALE A piece of paper that transfers the ownership of something from a seller to a buyer.

BILLET A term for the place where soldiers are quartered.

BINDER A temporary insurance policy covering the party applying for the insurance until the application can be approved by the home office of the insurance company.

BINDING ARBITRATION The taking of a dispute to an unbiased third party usually named by the disputing parties, who agree to be bound by the decisions made by the third party.

BLACKMAIL The illegal taking of money by threatening to injure a person's reputation or to expose some illegal action of the party being threatened.

BLACK-LETTER LAW A term for legal principles derived from statutes and cases that are recognized by the majority of judges in the country.

BLACK MARIA A popular name for an enclosed van used to transport prisoners.

BLANKET INSURANCE POLICY An insurance policy that covers more than one item or piece of property.

BLANKET MORTGAGE A mortgage covering more than one piece of property or building.

BLASPHEMY Speaking against God with the intent to incite contempt for the state religion.

BLOOD-GROUPING TEST A medical test that helps to determine the identity of the father of an illegitimate child.

BLOODHOUND A breed of dog possessing an exceptional ability to follow a scent; they are often used to track missing persons.

BLOTTER A book kept by the police that records the names of people who have been arrested.

BLUE-SKY LAWS A name given to laws that regulate the sale of shares of stock and other kinds of investments in order to protect the public from being cheated.

BNDD The abbreviation for the Bureau of Narcotics and Dangerous Drugs.

BODILY Having to do with the body.

BODILY REMAINS A corpse.

BOILERPLATE 1. A mass-produced legal form of a general type sold in stationery stores. 2. The parts of a contract that do not deal specifically with purpose of the contract; standardized contract provisions.

Bona fide In good faith; honest.

BONA FIDE PURCHASER Someone who purchases something in good faith; i.e., without knowing that a third party has a claim against the thing being purchased.

BOND 1. The proof of an existing debt, documented in writing. 2. A promise by a fiduciary to pay a certain sum if he does not perform his duties properly.

BONDED WAREHOUSE A building where imported goods are stored for a fee and where the duty on the goods doesn't have to be paid until they are removed from the warehouse.

BOOK VALUE The value of the assets of a business (as reflected in its account books) that relates to each share of a company's stock.

BOOTLEGGER A maker, seller, or transporter of illegal products, especially illegal whiskey.

BOOTLEGGING The manufacture, transportation, and sale of illegal products, especially illegal whiskey.

BOOTY The personal property of an enemy taken by the victors in a battle.

BOYCOTT The refusal of social or economic relations with a person, organization, or nation to punish or coerce that party to do something. The practice is named for Captain Boycott, an oppressive landlord in Ireland.

BREACH The violation of some law or duty.

BREACH OF CONTRACT Failure to perform an obligation arising out of a valid contract without a legal excuse. This excuses the other party from performing his obligation under the contract.

BREACH OF PEACE A broad term for describing conduct that intentionally disturbs the peace and tranquillity of a community.

BREACH OF PROMISE The breaking of a promise, especially a promise to marry.

BREAKING The act of destroying or separating property, usually for the purpose of illegally entering a building.

BRIBERY Giving, taking, or offering an illegal gift with the intent of influencing a public officer.

BRIEF 1. A written statement, of one side of an argument, that is submitted to a judge in a court proceeding. 2. An outline (of a case) that contains the facts, issues, and findings of the court that tried the case and the rationale behind the decision.

BROKER An agent in the business of selling, buying, or making contracts for items for his clients.

BROKERAGE HOUSE A company in the business of buying, selling, and making contracts for its customers.

BROTHEL A house of prostitution.

Brutum fulmen An idle threat.

BUGGERY Sexual intercourse between a human and a lower animal. Often used interchangeably with SODOMY. (See BESTIALITY.)

BUNCO GAME A trick or routine that is intended to deceive a person in order to obtain something of value from him.

BURDEN OF PROOF The duty to prove to a court the facts or issues under dispute. This does not shift during a trial. The term is also used to mean the burden of producing evidence; this burden does shift during the trial.

BURGLAR A person who commits the crime of burglary.

BURGLARY Defined in various statutes generally as the breaking and entering of a building with the intent to commit a felony.

BUYER 1. Someone who purchases something. 2. Someone who is employed by another for the purpose of buying merchandise.

BUYER-BROKER CONTRACTS Contracts between a broker and a party wanting to make a purchase.

BYLAWS Company rules governing its internal and external practices and interests.

◀ C ▶

CABINET A council that is assembled to give advice to the President.

CADAVER A dead human body.

CAHOOTS, IN In alliance or partnership.

CALABOOSE A jail or prison, from the Spanish word for dungeon, *calabozo*.

CALAMITY Great misfortune or disaster.

CALENDAR A docket, or schedule of cases to be tried in court.

CALLABLE BONDS Bonds whose payment may be called for before reaching maturity.

Calumnia, OR CALUMNY An antiquated term for falsely and maliciously accusing another person of a civil wrongdoing, now known as malicious prosecution.

CAMERALISTICS The business of collecting and spending public tax money.

CAMPBELL'S ACTS English laws that deal in prosecution for libel, awards of money to the relatives of persons killed by negligence, and restricting the sale of pornographic books. These laws have been widely copied by other countries.

CANCELLATION The act of revoking a contract.

Canfara Trial by hot iron.

CANON 1. A church dignitary. 2. A church law or rule. 3. A group of related laws.

CAPACITY Ability.

CAPACITY TO CONTRACT The legal ability to make a contract.

CAPITAL Money, especially that used in money-making ventures.

CAPITAL ASSET Generally, property held for investment,

whether or not for business purposes. The Internal Revenue Code defines the term very broadly.

CAPITAL GAIN Gain derived from the sale of a capital asset.

CAPITAL OFFENSE A major crime, for which an offender may face execution.

CAPITAL PUNISHMENT The punishment of being put to death.

CAPITAL STOCK Stock or shares in a corporation that are given in exchange for money invested.

CAPITALIZE To turn something into capital or money, for the purpose of making money.

CAPTION A part of a document that tells when, where, and under whose authority the document is executed.

CAPTIVES 1. Prisoners, especially prisoners of war. 2. Property taken from an enemy.

Carcer ad homines custodiendos, non ad puniendos, dari debet "A prison is for keeping prisoners, not punishing them."

CARE Attention; concern; caution.

CARGO Goods, merchandise, passengers, and freight carried by a ship, plane, train, or motor vehicle.

CARNAL KNOWLEDGE Sexual intercourse.

CARRIER A person, company, or corporation in the business of transporting people or things.

CARRIER'S LIEN The holding of freight until payment is made for having transported it.

CARRY COSTS Payment for expenses created by the party found at fault.

CARRYING AWAY Taking and removing; an element of the crime of larceny.

CARRYING WEAPONS The common-law offense of being armed with a weapon.

Carta A charter or a document.

CARTE BLANCHE 1. A blank check; a written instrument that

is signed but not completely filled out, allowing an agent to fill in whatever amount he sees fit. 2. Unlimited authority.

CARTEL An association or alliance of businesses all engaged in the same field of endeavor.

CASE A lawsuit that is taken to court.

CASE LAW Judgments already rendered on a legal issue, as opposed to statutes covering the subject.

CASH Money.

CASH SURRENDER VALUE Money raised when an insurance policy is cashed in with the issuer.

CASHIER'S CHECK A check made out by a bank, which promises to pay the amount of the check.

CASTIGATORY A ducking stool to which troublesome women were tied and then dunked into a pool of water as a form of punishment.

CASTLE DOCTRINE A doctrine stating that within the confines of one's home there is no duty to retreat from an aggressor in order to justify self-defense.

Casus fortuitus non est supponendus, et nemo tenetur divinare "One cannot be required to foresee an unexpected event."

CATTLE RUSTLING The stealing of cattle.

CAUSATION That which causes something to happen.

CAUSE OF ACTION 1. The wrongdoing with which a defendant is charged. 2. The facts that permit a cause to be tried and relief to be granted.

Caveat emptor "Let the buyer beware."

CEASE AND DESIST An order to stop, halt.

CERTAINTY That which is clear, distinct, and without doubt.

CERTIFICATE A written assurance that something has been or will be done.

CERTIFICATE OF DEPOSIT A bank's written acknowledgment of a deposit, with a promise to repay it, when so ordered, to the depositor or some other person designated by the depositor.

CERTIFICATE OF STOCK A document declaring that a named person owns a specified number of shares in a corporation.

CERTIFIED CHECK A check that is guaranteed by a bank to be good.

CERTIORARI A re-examination of the findings of an inferior court by an appellate court, the purpose of which is to obtain more information or to determine if there was a miscarriage of justice by the lower court.

CHAMBERS A judge's office.

CHAMPERTY An illegal agreement between a party to a lawsuit and a third person in which the third person agrees to take over the suit at his expense for a share of any recovery in the suit.

CHAMPERTOUS Having to do with the crime of champerty.

CHANCELLOR A judge in a court of equity.

CHANGE OF VENUE Holding a trial in another location, usually because a fair trial would be impossible in the county where the incident in question occurred, but sometimes for reasons of convenience.

CHAPTER ELEVEN The chapter in the UNIFORM COMMERCIAL CODE (U.C.C.) that enables a court to arrange the payments of a debtor's obligations during the course of a bankruptcy.

CHARACTER The sum of the qualities that can be attributed to a person, place, or thing.

Chargé d'affaires (Fr.) A low-ranking diplomatic officer.

CHARITABLE CORPORATION An organization that gives free charitable services.

CHARLATAN The old word for a quack or a fake.

Carta de non ente non valet "A deed for a piece of property that doesn't exist is not a valid deed."

CHARTER 1. A document that defines and grants some authority. 2. A certificate, incorporating some business or organization, given by a state. 3. The hiring of some mode of transportation.

CHARTER PARTY A party that hires, by a written contract, a

bus, airplane, train, or ship for the duration of a certain trip.

CHATTEL A piece of property other than land or a building; personal property, including an animal.

CHATTEL MORTGAGE A written document that transfers title of an article of personal property to another as security for some debt.

CHEAT 1. The act of intentionally deceiving, defrauding, or swindling. 2. A person who intentionally deceives, defrauds, or swindles.

CHECK A signed instrument, by a customer of a bank, requesting that money be paid out of his account to another.

CHILD ABANDONMENT The neglect or relinquishment of parental duties.

CHILD LABOR LAWS Those laws which prevent the exploitation of children as workers.

CHILD SUPPORT An allowance paid by one divorced spouse to the other for the financial support of their children.

CHOSE An article of personal property.

CHOSE IN ACTION Personal property that is not in the possession of its owner but that the owner has the right to possess.

CHOSE IN POSSESSION Personal property in the possession of its owner.

CHIEF JUSTICE The highest-ranking judge of a court.

C.I.F. On an invoice, this means that the quoted price includes *cost, insurance, and freight* to a designated location.

CIRCUIT COURT A court having jurisdiction over a large territory comprising several towns or districts and that must travel to hear cases in each district.

CIRCUIT JUDGE A judge in a circuit court.

CIRCUMSTANTIAL EVIDENCE Information that is the result of reasoning, not hard facts. It is indirect evidence; that is, it is the basis from which a fact at issue must be inferred.

CITATION 1. An order to appear in court on a specified day. 2. Bibliographic information that follows a case name so that the court transcripts may be looked up for additional information about the decision.

CITE 1. To order (a person) to appear in court; issue a citation. 2. Give bibliographic information about a case.

CIVIL ACTION A lawsuit for the purpose of protecting a person's civil rights or obtaining damages for their violation.

CIVIL DEATH The loss of one's civil rights.

CIVIL LAW The law of the continent of Europe as originated from Roman law.

CIVIL RIGHTS Those rights defined by law and belonging to the citizens of a country. Examples: property rights, freedom of contract, freedom from unwanted physical intrusions.

Civiliter mortuus Civilly dead; a term that describes a person who has had his civil rights taken away as a form of punishment.

CLAIM A demand.

CLAIM JUMPING The stealing of mining claims by staking one's own claim on the same piece of property where another claim exists, or by force.

CLAIMANT A person who claims something, especially an inheritance or a tax refund.

Clam delinquentes magis puniuntur quam palam "Those who secretly sin are punished more severely than those who sin openly."

CLANDESTINE Secret; hidden; concealed.

CLANDESTINE OPERATION A secret mission or activity.

CLASS ACTION A lawsuit waged on behalf of others with identical claims or complaints, usually where each individual's recovery would be too small to make an individual suit practical.

CLASS SUIT A class action.

CLASSIFICATION OF RISKS A term for the part of an insurance policy that specifies which types of risks are covered by the policy.

Clausum fregit He broke the close, meaning that an accused trespasser entered where he had no right to enter.

CLEAN HANDS A doctrine that denies relief to a plaintiff because of his misconduct in the matter.

CLEAR AND CONVINCING PROOF Evidence that is easily understood and believable beyond a reasonable doubt.

CLEAR AND PRESENT DANGER Serious immediate violence that can be expected to occur.

CLEAR TITLE A title to property that is free from limitations or claims by others.

CLERKSHIP The time spent by a law-school graduate working in the office of a practicing lawyer or judge. A clerk usually helps a judge write opinions.

CLIENT A person who hires an attorney.

CLOSE CORPORATION A corporation in which directors and officers can fill vacancies in their number without consulting the stockholders.

CLOSED SEASON A period of time during the year when a particular species of fish or game is protected from all hunting.

CLOSED SESSION A meeting of a legislature or a court which is not open to the public.

CLOUD ON TITLE A claim against a title of land, whether the claim is valid or not.

CO. The abbreviation for company.

COADMINISTRATOR A person who shares the duties of an administrator with another.

COEXECUTOR A person sharing the duties of an executor with another.

COALITION A group of people who agree to act together if mutual demands are not met.

COAST GUARD A military or naval force whose duties include enforcing maritime laws, defending the coast, and protecting life and property at sea.

C.O.D. On an invoice, these letters indicate that the deliverer of an item will *collect* the price *on delivery*.

CODE A collection of laws.

CODE OF CRIMINAL PROCEDURE A collection of laws governing the method by which a suspected criminal is tried.

CODE OF HONOR The written laws that govern dueling.

Code Napoléon The laws that governed Napoleon's empire, many of which still survive in Europe.

CODEX A code or collection of laws.

CODICIL A written supplement or modification to a will, which must be executed with the same formalities as the will.

COERCION The forcing of another, through physical force or threat, to do something he would not otherwise do.

COGNIZANCE Awareness or recognition, often used in reference to a judge's acknowledgment and acceptance of some matter.

COGNOVIT A defendant's written confession admitting the truth of the charges brought against him, allowing a judgment to be entered against him.

COHABITATION The state of living together as husband and wife.

COLD-BLOODED MURDER Willful, premeditated homicide.

COLLATERAL ATTACK An attempt to make void, in a separate action, a valid judgment on some issue at court.

COLLATERAL ESTOPPEL A court's prevention of a person from making a claim in court that has already been proved true or false.

COLLATERAL SECURITY Anything of value, especially items of personal property, used to insure the repayment of a loan in addition to the personal obligation to repay.

COLLECTION AGENCY A company in the business of collecting delinquent bills for their clients.

COLLISION The crashing together of objects.

COLLUSION A secret agreement or combination between two or more persons to commit some improper act. It often describes persons with ostensibly conflicting interests who use legal proceedings to deceive a court or its officers.

COLOR The *prima facie* appearance of something.

COMBAT A violent struggle or duel between two or more people.

COMITY Courtesy; granting of a privilege out of good will and not as a right. Used to describe the effect courts of one state give to decisions and statutes of another state.

COMITY OF NATIONS The recognition of one nation's law by another nation.

Commercia belli Contracts of war; contracts made between warring nations, such as prisoner exchanges, cease-fire agreements, letters of safe conduct, etc.

COMMERCIAL INSOLVENCY The inability of a business to pay its debts.

COMMERCIAL LAW The area of law that concerns itself with persons engaged in business.

COMMERCIAL PAPER Negotiable instruments, checks, notes, and bills of exchange.

COMMISSION 1. A written authorization issued by the government to an individual, organization, or group of people. 2. A payment based on a fraction of a gross profit. 3. The doing of a criminal act.

COMMITTEE A guardian appointed to care for the person and property of an incompetent.

COMMODATUM A contract to return a borrowed article by a certain time.

COMMODITY Movable goods that are bought, sold, or traded.

COMMON LAW 1. A system of law originating in medieval England. 2. Case law, as opposed to statute law.

COMMUNICATE To impart, share, or make known.

COMMUNITY PROPERTY A concept in some states whereby property acquired during marriage is jointly owned by husband and wife. Separate property ownership is still possible in these states, however.

COMPACT A formal contract between two governments.

COMPARATIVE NEGLIGENCE When both parties in a tort action have been found to be at fault, the doctrine of comparative negligence allows the less negligent to recover proportionate damages.

COMPARATIVE RECTITUDE The doctrine that grants a divorce to the spouse found to be the less at fault when both spouses are found at fault.

COMPATIBILITY The ability of two people, especially spouses, to get along.

COMPEL To force.

COMPENSATION Payment or benefit given, or work performed, for an injury or loss suffered.

COMPETENCY PROCEEDING A judicial proceeding to determine if one is mentally able to manage one's own affairs.

COMPETENT Able; authorized; qualified. Often used to mean mental capacity to understand one's acts.

COMPLAINANT A party who files a complaint.

COMPLAINT The initial pleading by a plaintiff in a civil action.

COMPLICE A partner in crime.

Compos mentis Mental soundness; competence.

COMPOSITION A formal, written agreement, usually settling debts for less than the actual amount due.

COMPOUND INTEREST Interest computed on interest already earned.

COMPOUNDING A FELONY (A victim's) taking payment for not prosecuting a crime suffered. This is itself a crime.

Comprivigni Children by a previous marriage.

COMPROMISE The settlement of a dispute by the making of mutual concessions by the parties.

COMPULSION A force that makes someone do something he would not otherwise have done.

COMPULSORY Forced; mandatory.

COMPURGATORS Neighbors of a defendant who appear in court to say that they believe the defendant's innocence.

CON The abbreviation used for: 1. A confidence man. 2. The confidence game. 3. A convicted criminal.

CONCEALED Hidden; withheld.

CONCEALED WEAPON A weapon that is kept hidden on the person.

CONCEALING STOLEN PROPERTY The criminal offense of knowingly hiding stolen property.

CONCEALMENT The hiding of material facts from one who should be told. This is a type of fraud.

CONCERT OF ACTION An agreed-upon act.

CONCURRENT JURISDICTION A situation in which two courts are empowered to try the same cases.

CONDEMN 1. To find guilty. 2. To seize private property for public use.

CONDEMNATION The seizure of private property for public use.

CONDITION A restriction or limitation on conduct; or a future event upon which an act is made to depend.

CONDITIONAL Depending on terms not yet made.

CONDITIONAL SALE A sale in which a buyer must meet certain terms before taking full possession.

CONDITIONS OF SALE The terms of a sale.

CONDOMINIUM 1. Private ownership of a unit in a multiunit building. 2. A multiunit building with each unit being owned by private party.

CONDONATION The pardoning by a marital partner of the misconduct of a spouse, thereby barring future divorce proceedings for that misconduct.

CONDUCT 1. Personal behavior. 2. To lead or direct.

CONFEDERACY An association organized for the purpose of violating the law.

CONFEDERATION An alliance of nations or states.

CONFESSION An accused person's admission of guilt.

CONFESSION OF JUDGMENT A judgment based on the written confession of a debtor.

CONFIDENCE Trust.

CONFIDENCE GAME A trick used to obtain money from unsuspecting persons; a swindle.

CONFIDENCE MAN A person who tricks people into giving him their money; a swindler.

CONFIDENTIAL COMMUNICATIONS Statements made in private between two parties, with the assumption that the statements will not be passed on to third parties. These statements are protected against investigation by the courts. Example: communication between a doctor and his patient.

CONFIDENTIAL RELATIONSHIP A relationship based on the trust that statements made by one party will not be disclosed by the other. Examples: attorney and client; husband and wife.

CONFIRMATION The validation of a contract, which provides proof of the existence of the contract.

CONFISCATION The seizure of private property without compensation to the owner.

CONFLICT OF LAWS A difference between the laws of the states affecting a lawsuit between the citizens of those states.

CONFRONTATION 1. The facing of the accused by a witness or accuser during a criminal trial. 2. The cross-examination of a witness.

CONJUGAL RIGHTS Rights arising out of a marital relationship; most often, the right to love and companionship that one spouse expects from the other.

CONNIVANCE Passive consent to or guilty knowledge of some crime; intentional failure to prevent a wrong.

CONSANGUINITY The relationship between two persons descending from the same ancestor.

CONSCRIPTION The practice of drafting people into the military services.

CONSENSUAL CONTRACT A contract that is formed by the mere consenting of the contracting parties, without written evidence.

CONSENT Agree; comply; approve.

CONSERVATOR A caretaker appointed by a judge to manage property belonging to a person unable to manage it by himself.

CONSIDERATION Something of value given in exchange for performance or a promise by another party. Consideration of some sort is the basis for all contracts.

CONSIGNEE A person who sells goods on consignment.

CONSIGNMENT The practice of handing over property or goods to another for the purpose of selling them, yet retaining ownership of the goods until they are sold.

CONSIGNOR A person for whom goods are sold on consignment.

CONSORTIUM 1. The marital duties and obligations that one spouse owes another. 2. An international business or banking agreement.

CONSPIRACY An unlawful alliance between two or more persons for the purpose of committing a crime. If one is in on the planning of a crime, one can be held responsible for the later criminal action even if one takes no part in it. The planning must be combined with some overt act seeking to accomplish the criminal purpose in order for conspiracy to be established.

CONSPIRATOR A person who commits the crime of conspiracy.

CONSTABLE 1. policeman. 2. A sheriff's deputy assigned to a particular locality.

CONSTITUTION The basic laws of a nation, establishing the government, defining the rights of its citizens, and defining the powers of the government.

CONSTITUTIONAL LAW An area of the law that deals with the interpretation of and compliance with the constitution.

CONSTITUTIONAL RIGHT A right that is guaranteed to the citizens of a nation by its constitution.

CONSTRUCTIVE That which is not actual or physical but is accepted by the law as a substitute. A constructive eviction, for example, would be some activity, such as turning off the electricity, by a landlord intending to oust a tenant.

CONSTRUCTIVE BREAKING The breaking element of burglary ("breaking and entering"), which can be satisfied even though the burglar doesn't actually break anything in order to make his entrance.

CONSTRUCTIVE DESERTION A situation in which one spouse forces the other spouse to leave, so that the remaining spouse is the actual deserter.

Consuetudo curiae The custom of the court.

Consuetudo loci observanda est "The customs of a locality are to be observed."

CONSUMER A person who pays money for anything obtained for his personal use.

CONSUMER PROTECTION The area of the law that protects people who pay money for goods and services from being placed in unfair bargaining positions, from injury from unsafe merchandise and from misrepresentation by a seller. (See PRODUCT LIABILITY.)

CONSUMMATION OF MARRIAGE The fulfillment of a marriage by sexual relations between the bride and groom.

CONTEMPT A rude disregard or defiance (of a public authority).

CONTEMPT OF COURT Rudeness or disobedience to a judge during the course of a trial, or outside of court if a court order is disobeyed.

CONTINGENT FEE An attorney's fee based on a percentage of what his client recovers in a suit.

CONTINUING TRESPASS An unlawful act, or a lawful act carried out in an unlawful manner, that permanently invades the property of another. Example: building a house on your own property in such a way that it overhangs your neighbor's land is a continuing trespass.

Contra Against, in answer to, or in opposition to.

CONTRABAND 1. Those goods of which the importation, the exportation, or the possession is illegal. 2. Goods that a neutral nation is forbidden by international law to carry to a warring nation.

CONTRACT An agreement or promise between two or more parties to do or not to do a bargained-for act in exchange for consideration.

CONTRACT LAW The area of law that deals in the formation and enforcement of contracts.

CONTRACT REMEDY A relief available to a party suffering from damages resulting from a contract that hasn't been fulfilled.

CONTRACT RIGHT A right that has been contracted for.

CONTRIBUTING TO THE DELIQUENCY OF A MINOR Assisting the criminality or immorality of a minor.

CONTRIBUTION 1. The sharing of a loss or debt by two or more parties. 2. A donation.

CONTRIBUTORY The joining of two or more parties in responsibility for some act.

CONTRIBUTORY NEGLIGENCE A plaintiff's negligent conduct (or lack of ordinary care) that adds to the negligence of another and results in the plaintiff's injury. This is a partial defense to a charge of negligence on the defendant's part.

CONVERSION The unlawful exercise of ownership over property belonging to another.

CONVEYANCE 1. The transfer of title to property (usually real property) from one party to another. 2. A written instrument transferring title of property from one party to another.

CONVICT A person who has been found guilty of a crime.

CONVICTION The finding (of a criminal defendant) to be guilty as charged.

COOLING-OFF PERIOD A period of time to rethink a course of action, used especially in labor strikes when the union continues on the job while negotiations continue.

COPYRIGHT The exclusive ownership of and right to publish literary or other artistic works.

Coram nobis A writ to bring some error or fact to the attention of a court.

CORONER A public officer charged with investigating the cause of deaths occurring within his or her jurisdiction.

CORONER'S INQUEST A coroner's investigation of the circumstances surrounding a death suspected to be caused by foul play.

CORP. The abbreviation for corporation.

CORPORAL PUNISHMENT Physical punishment.

CORPORATE law The area of the law dealing with the formation and operation of corporations.

CORPORATE PERKS (PERQUISITES) Benefits, provided to business executives, that are not included in a salary and on which income taxes are not paid (although this is changing); for example, the use of a company-owned airplane or automobile would be considered a corporate perk.

CORPORATION A business owned by shareholders whose liability for acts of the corporation is limited to the amount of their investment. A corporation is an artificial person and is created and operates under state law.

Corpus delicti The body of the crime; the proof that a crime has been committed. Examples: A murdered man's body; the charred remains of a house.

Corpus juris The body of the law; a compilation of the law.

CORRUPT CONSENT Consent given unlawfully.

COSTS Fees for the defense and prosecution of a party in court; often recoverable from the losing party.

COTENANCY The undivided ownership of something by more than one person.

COUNSEL An attorney who represents a client in court.

COURSE OF DEALING The conduct of the parties prior to the formation of a contract.

COUNT Each claim or charge constituting a criminal indictment or civil complaint.

COUNTERCLAIM A claim by a defendant, connected with the matter introduced by the plaintiff, attempting to reduce the damages claimed by the plaintiff.

COUNTERFEIT 1. That which is unlawfully forged, copied, or imitated with the intent to deceive or defraud. 2. To unlawfully forge, copy, or imitate with the intent to deceive or defraud.

COUNTERFEITING The act of unlawfully forging, copying, or imitating something with the intent to deceive or defraud.

COUNTEROFFER An offer made by an offeree in response to an offer by an offeror that changes the terms of the original offer; must be agreed to by the original offeror.

COURT A place where justice is administered under the direction of one or more judges.

COURT COSTS The price paid for going to court to defend or maintain a claim.

COURT OF APPEALS A court in which appeals are heard.

COUPLED WITH AN INTEREST A term describing an agent who has an interest in the property that is the subject of the agency, beyond a salary or profits from acting as an agent.

COURT OF CLAIMS A court in which claims against the federal government are heard; some states also have courts of claim.

COURT OF BANKRUPTCY A federal district court's jurisdiction over matters arising out of bankruptcy.

COVENANT 1. An agreement or contract, written or implied, within a deed to real property. 2. Any agreement reduced to writing. Example: an agreement not to compete with a former employer in a certain town.

COVERT Hidden, undercover, or protected by a disguise.

COVERTURE The status of a married woman, under the protection of her husband.

CREDIT 1. The reliability of a borrower of money or a buyer of goods on time. 2. The esteem by which a person is held in society. 3. Something of monetary value.

CREDITOR A person who is owed money.

CREDITOR'S BILL A lawsuit by a creditor who is unable to collect what is owed to him.

CRIME 1. Any act that violates a penal law. 2. Any offense against the public.

CRIMINAL CAPACITY The ability of a person to do a criminal act.

CRIMINAL CONVERSATION Sexual intercourse with the spouse of another; adultery.

CRIMINIAL HOMICIDE Murder.

CRIMINAL INFORMATION A criminal suit brought outside the grand-jury system by a prosecuting attorney.

CRIMINAL INTENT An element of crime; the intent or desire of a suspect to deliberately commit a crime.

CRIMINAL LAW The area of the law concerned with crimes and the punishment of criminals.

CRIMINAL NEGLIGENCE A wanton, willful, and grossly negligent act showing reckless disregard for the rights of others and deserving of criminal blame.

CRIMINAL NONSUPPORT The crime of failing to provide for the financial needs of one's ex-wife and children.

CROSS CLAIM A defendant's claim brought in retaliation against the plaintiff in the same action to obtain full relief for the parties or to aid in defense of the original claim.

CROSS COMPLAINT A counterclaim; a charge or claim made by a defendant against the plaintiff.

CROSS-EXAMINATION The questioning of a witness for one side by the other side in court in order to test his evidence. This follows direct examination of the witness.

CRUEL AND UNUSUAL PUNISHMENT Those kinds of punishments forbidden by the constitution; specifically, torture.

CULPABLE At fault, or deserving of blame.

CURTESY The right of a man to property owned by his late wife.

CURTILAGE The physical area immediately surrounding a household.

CUSTODY 1. Care. 2. Detention.

CUSTOM An unwritten law or practice established by usage over a long period of time.

◂ D ▸

DAMAGE Some injury to a person, his reputation, or his property that results from a wrongful act by another, an accident, or negligence.

DAMAGE FEASANT Damage done to land by animals.

DAMAGES Money awarded by a court to someone who has been wrongfully injured.

Damnatus Unlawful.

Damnatus coitus Unlawful sexual intercourse.

Damnum Damages or loss.

Damnum absque injuria Damages without injury in the legal sense and therefore not afforded a legal remedy.

DANGEROUS PER SE Dangerous in itself, such as dynamite or cyanide.

Dans et retinens, nihil dat "Retaining possession of something you give to another is not a gift."

DAY IN COURT A person's right to be heard in court and defend himself.

DAYSMAN An elected judge or arbitrator.

De bene esse Conditionally; for the time being.

De bonis propriis A court's finding against an administrator or executor of an estate requiring the party to pay, out of his own pocket, money taken from the estate.

De dote unde nihil habet A court's decision to give part of a husband's estate to his widow when nothing in the will is left for her.

De estroveriis habendis An old term for a court's decision to grant alimony to an ex-wife.

De facto In fact.

De homine replegande A court's order to remove a man

from prison or to take him from the custody of a private institution or custodian.

De jure Legitimate, lawful.

De lunatico inquirendo A court's inquiry as to whether a defendant is or is not insane.

De minimis non curat lex "The law is not concerned with insignificant, unessential matters."

De novo Anew; afresh.

DEADLY FORCE Force that is likely to cause death.

DEADLY WEAPON Any instrument used in a manner that could cause death.

DEBAUCHERY A broad term descriptive of sexual immorality in excess of what is lawful.

DEBENTURE An unsecured corporate debt, usually on an interest-bearing bond.

Debet esse finis litum "There should be an end to litigation."

Debita sequuntur personam debitoris "Debts follow a person in debt"; a debt cannot be escaped by moving away, and can be collected wherever a debtor is found.

DEBIT A bookkeeper's term for a sum that is owed.

DEBT Money owed.

DEBTOR A person who owes money to another.

DECAPITATION A form of capital punishment, still used in some parts of the world, whereby the victim's head is cut off.

DECEDENT A dead person.

DECEIT The act of willfully misleading, or withholding information, in order to cause injury to another.

DECENCY The proper speech, dress, and actions requisite for lawful conduct.

Decipi quam fallere est tutius "To be deceived is safer than to be a deceiver"; a deceived person can seek a remedy in court, while a deceiver will have a hard time defending himself.

DECLARANT A person who makes a formal statement, or declaration.

DECLARATION 1. A public proclamation. 2. A statement made out of court regarding some fact. 3. A formal statement.

DECLARATION OF INTENT An alien's formal renouncing of allegiance to his former government or sovereign in order to become a citizen of the United States.

DECLARATORY JUDGMENT A judicial statement answering a legal question asked by a party or parties involved in some matter that might have legal consequences. No actual wrong need yet have been committed, and the judgment does not order that anything be done.

DECREE An announcement of a court's decision and the legal remedy ordered to correct the situation.

DEDITION The giving up, or relinquishing, of something.

DEED A written document intended to transfer the ownership of real property to another.

DEFALCATION The failure to account properly for funds, especially by the administrator or executor of an estate.

DEFAMATION Injury to the reputation of another for which an action for damages may be brought. Libel and slander are types of defamation.

DEFAME To do injury to the reputation (of another).

DEFAULT 1. Failure to perform a required act during the course of a lawsuit. 2. Failure to fulfill an obligation or perform a legal duty.

DEFAULT JUDGMENT A judgment against a party in a lawsuit who fails to file certain papers required by the court.

DEFECT 1. A flaw, imperfection, or failing. 2. To forsake one's country.

DEFENDANT The party that acts to defend itself against the charges of the plaintiff or prosecutor in court.

DEFENDANT IN ERROR The winner of a lawsuit who gets hauled back into court by the losers, who hope to have the decision of the court overturned.

DEFENSE Those reasons, offered to the court by the defendant, that argue against the charges brought forth by the plaintiff or prosecution.

DEFENSE OF HABITATION A term for those acts that are undertaken in the defense of a person's residence against an intruder. There is greater justification for using violence in this situation than in other types of confrontation.

DEFENSE OF OTHERS A term for those acts undertaken in the defense of other people.

DEFENSE OF PROPERTY A term for those acts undertaken to defend one's property from injury, destruction, or theft by the acts of another.

DEFERRED PAYMENTS Postponed payments, as in an installment plan.

DEFINITIVE Final.

DEFORCEMENT The keeping of land from its rightful possessor.

DEFORCER A person who unlawfully possesses a piece of land, keeping a party with lawful right off the property.

DEGREES OF MURDER Murders are classified by "types" or degrees, which are determined by the guilt of the defendant at the time of a homicide. For example, a first-degree of murder must be willful, deliberate and premeditated, or committed in the attempt to carry out a felony.

Dei gratia By the grace of God.

Del credere A guarantee, given by an agent to someone whose goods the agent sells, that the buyer will pay the full price.

DELEGATE A person who is elected to represent a group.

DELEGATION A group of representatives.

DELEGATION OF DUTY The transfer of duty or authority from one person to another.

Delegata potestas non potest delegari "A delegated power cannot be delegated"; since a delegate has been elected especially to represent a group, he cannot appoint someone else to do his job without the group's permission.

Delictum A civil or criminal wrong; a tort.

DELINQUENT 1. (A debt that is) due and unpaid. 2. A person who is negligent in his financial obligations. 3. A minor who has broken the law.

Delirium tremens A disorder of the nervous system that produces temporary attacks of insanity, usually resulting from excessive consumption of alcohol.

DELIVERY The transfer of something from one place or party to another.

DELUSION 1. That which is based upon a falsehood. 2. Hallucinations arising from some physical or mental disorder.

DEMAND A claim or request.

DEMAND NOTE A check or note that is payable when presented to the proper party, rather than at a specific time.

DEMISE 1. Death. 2. The transferral of property from one person to another. 3. The lease of some real property.

DEMUR A formal objection.

DEMURRER A plea made in court that the opponent's alleged facts, if true, would not support the opponent's argument.

DENIZEN A resident.

DEPARTMENT OF DEFENSE (DOD) A federal organization regulating and administering the military services.

DEPARTMENT OF TRANSPORTATION (DOT) A federal organization regulating and administrating matters of transportation.

DEPONENT A person who testifies under oath outside the courtroom and whose testimony is written down for the purpose of being presented in a trial.

DEPORTATION The expulsion of an alien from a country.

DEPOSE 1. To give testimony in writing, under oath. 2. To remove (a person) from public office.

DEPOSIT 1. Money or property that is released to another as security for a loan and that will be returned to its owner after the loan is settled. 2. Money put into a bank account. 3. Goods temporarily given to another for safekeeping.

FEDERAL DEPOSIT INSURANCE ACT An act insuring money against loss when deposited in banks eligible for the insurance. There is a uniform limit on the amount of insurance on each bank account.

DEPOSITION 1. Sworn testimony, in writing, taken from a witness outside the courtroom. 2. The process of taking sworn testimonies outside the courtroom.

DEPRECIATION An allowance for the wear and tear and service of possessions.

DEPUTY A person authorized to take the place of or assist a superior officer, especially a sheriff or a cabinet member.

DERELICT 1. Abandoned. 2. No longer in use. 3. (n.) A tramp, hobo, bum.

DEROGATE To diminish; lessen; belittle.

DESCENDANT A person who follows in the lineage of an ancestor. Examples: a child, grandchild.

DESCENT The acquiring of an estate through inheritance.

DESCRIPTION A written or verbal portrait of a person, place, thing, or act.

Descriptio personae A word or phrase, descriptive of a person's identity, within a written instrument.

DESERTION The intentional abandonment of an obligation, duty, or property, particularly in reference to a husband who abandons his wife.

DETAINER The act of withholding property against the will of a person lawfully entitled to it.

DETERMINABLE Able to be decided or settled.

DETINUE An antiquated term for a court action to recover goods or their value from a party accused of wrongfully taking, using, or damaging goods belonging to another.

Devastavit The mismanagement of a decedent's estate by an executor, resulting in waste or loss to the estate.

DEVIATION Generally, a departure from proper conduct.

DEVISE A gift of real property by will.

DICTUM A discussion by the court of something that does not pertain directly to the outcome of the case being tried.

DIGEST A set of books containing summaries or abstracts, of previous court decisions, which help lawyers to find precedents.

DILATORY Intentionally causing or attempting to cause a delay.

DILIGENCE Persistence; alertness; care.

DIMINISHED CAPACITY A mental defect or disease that prevents a person from knowing the difference between right and wrong.

DIRECT CONTEMPT Conduct in a courtroom that embarrasses the judge or hinders justice.

DIRECT EVIDENCE Definite proof of a fact without the intervention of proof of another fact. (See CIRCUMSTANTIAL EVIDENCE.)

DIRECT EXAMINATION The questioning of a witness in court by the party presenting the witness to the court, as opposed to cross-examination.

DIRECTOR A fiduciary elected by stockholders to manage the affairs of a corporation.

DISALLOW To not allow; to reject or deny.

DISBARMENT The taking away of a lawyer's license to practice law, because of unprofessional or illegal conduct.

DISCHARGE The release from a contractual obligation, debt, or confinement.

DISCLAIMER The rejection or renouncing of a claim, right, or privilege.

DISCLOSURE The open declaration of something that is secret.

DISCOUNT A deduction from a gross sum.

DISCOVERY Pretrial procedures in which opposing parties may obtain and exchange information regarding the factual dispute of the trial. Each party seeks information that it needs and that the other party alone has.

DISCREDIT 1. To cast doubt upon the reputation of a witness. 2. To refuse to believe.

DISFRANCHISE To deprive another of a right.

DISHONOR The refusal to pay or accept a negotiable instrument when it becomes due.

DISINHERIT To deprive one's heirs from obtaining all or part of one's estate.

DISMISS To throw (a case) out of court.

DISORDERLY CONDUCT A broad term for any act by a person that would disturb the order of the community.

DISORDERLY HOUSE 1. A house whose residents practice such bad behavior that the household becomes a nuisance to the surrounding neighborhood. 2. A house of prostitution.

DISPARAGE To maliciously discredit or degrade a person, his goods, or his real property.

DISPENSATION Permission to do something that would otherwise be illegal.

DISPUTE A controversy about some fact.

DISSENTING OPINION An opinion of a judge that disagrees with the decision of the majority of judges who heard the same case.

DISSOLUTION The nullification, or cancellation, of a legal proceeding or a corporate, contractual, or marital relationship.

DISTRAIN To take goods belonging to a debtor without first going to court in order to force payment of the debt.

DISTRESS The practice of taking a person's possessions in order to force the payment of a debt.

DISTRICT A political area with distinct boundaries.

DISTRICT ATTORNEY A lawyer whose job is to prosecute persons accused of violating the law within a court's district and to represent the government in civil actions.

DIVERSITY A prisoner's plea that he has actually been mistaken for a real criminal. This is a question of identity, not of guilt.

DIVERSITY OF CITIZENSHIP A situation existing when the opposing parties in a lawsuit live in different states.

DIVEST To take a right or interest from a person who was originally entitled to the right or interest. (Also "devest.")

DIVIDEND 1. A division of the gross profits of a corporation paid out to shareholders. 2. The accumulated interest accrued by a savings account during a given time.

DIVINE LAW The law of God.

DIVISIBLE CONTRACT A contract, consisting of several individual parts not necessarily dependent on each other, in which the breaching of one part will not cause the breaching party to be liable for the breach of the entire contract.

DIVISION OF OPINION A disagreement, among a panel of judges hearing a case, that prevents them from deciding the case.

DIVORCE The judicial dissolution of a marriage.

DIVORCE *a mensa et thoro* A divorce to the extent that the parties are forbidden to live together, although the marriage continues.

DIVORCE *a vinculo matrimonii* The total and complete dissolution of a marriage.

DOCK The place in a courtroom where the prisoner sits or stands during the trial.

DOCKET A schedule, or list, of cases soon to be tried.

DOCTRINE A principle, or rule, of law.

DOCUMENT A written record.

DOCUMENT OF TITLE A document that serves as proof of ownership.

DOING BUSINESS A broad term describing the pursuit of financial livelihood or gain.

Doli capax The ability or capacity to tell the difference between right and wrong.

Doli incapax The inability or incapacity to tell the difference between right and wrong.

Dolosus versatur in generalibus "Deceivers speak in generalities."

DOMAIN Property under the rule or influence of another country.

DOMESTIC 1. A broad term for things that have to do with a household. 2. Things pertaining to a nation.

DOMICILE A permanent home—as opposed to a residence, which may be temporary.

DOMINION Control or ownership.

Domus sua cuique est tutissimum refugium "A person's home is his safest refuge."

Dona clandestina sunt semper suspiciosa "Secret gifts are always suspicious."

DONATIVE TRUST A trust that has been set up and presented as a gift.

DONEE A person to whom some thing or power is given by a donor.

DONOR A person who gives some thing or power to someone else (the donee).

DORMANT Inactive.

DORMANT PARTNER A partner who does not take an active role in the running of a business.

Dormiunt aliquando leges, nunquam moriuntur "The law might languish or relax, but it will never die."

DOSSIER A collection of papers on a particular subject.

DOUBLE JEOPARDY Being tried more than once for the same crime. It is forbidden by the Constitution.

DOWAGER A widow in possession of her late husband's estate.

DOWER A wife's right to her deceased husband's property (now rare).

DRAFT A written order for payment of money. Example: a check.

DRAM SHOP A saloon where liquor is sold by the drink.

DRAWEE A person or bank requested to pay out money for a bill or withdrawal. Example: the bank where someone writing a check has a checking account.

DRAWER The person who requests a drawee to pay out money. Example: Someone who writes a check.

DRAWLATCHES Robbers; thieves.

Droit (Fr.) 1. Justice; law. 2. Right.

DRUG ADDICTION The state of physical and mental dependence on a drug or drugs.

DRUNKENNESS The condition of a person who is under the influence of liquor.

DUAL CITIZENSHIP The status of a person who is the citizen of two countries at the same time.

Duces tecum A writ ordering a person to appear in court and to bring a specified thing with him to be used as evidence in the trial.

DUE That for which the time has come.

DUE BILL A written acknowledgment of a debt.

DUE CARE The care taken by a reasonable and ordinarily prudent man in any particular circumstance, to the extent demanded by the circumstance.

DUE PROCESS OF LAW The rules and principles established in our judicial system for the safeguarding of individual rights such as the right to argue in defense of charges brought against one.

DUEL A fight between two persons at an appointed time and place for the purpose of illegally settling an argument or a slur upon the honor of one or both of the combatants.

DUNGEON An underground prison or cell.

Duo non possunt in solido unam rem possidere "Two people cannot each own the same thing in its entirety."

DUPLICITY Uniting two or more causes of action or defenses in one plea; generally, deception or double-dealing.

DURESS The unlawful forcing of another in order to make that person perform an act he would normally not have done.

DUTCH AUCTION An auction at which the bidding is started

at a higher price than the goods are worth, then lowered until matched by a bidder.

DUTY 1. That which is done in order to secure compliance with a law or with someone else's right. 2. A tax.

DUTY TO MITIGATE DAMAGES The duty owed to a defendant by the plaintiff not to exaggerate the damages being sought, or to take advantage of circumstances to lessen the damages suffered. Example: When a party refuses to purchase items he's agreed to buy, the seller should try to sell the items again before making the original buyer liable for the full price.

DWELLING The residence of a person or persons.

DYER ACT A statute making the transportation of a stolen motor vehicle across state lines a federal crime.

DYSNOMY Bad law.

◂ E ▸

Ea intentione With that intent.

EARMARK 1. A mark that distinguishes one animal from others. 2. Commonly, to say that money or funds are earmarked for a certain purpose means that money has already been set aside for that purpose.

EARN To obtain or acquire something, especially money, in exchange for work.

EARNED INCOME Income from work; wages.

EARNER A person who works for an income, either by working for himself or for someone else.

EARNEST MONEY A partial payment for goods made in order to bind the seller to a contract for the sale of the goods.

EARNINGS 1. Money obtained through labor. 2. The price paid for doing a job.

EARNING POWER A person's ability to obtain money.

EARWITNESS A witness who gives testimony as to what he has heard.

EASEMENT A right to use a piece of land belonging to another in a particular way. Example: a way over a neighbor's land to get to a beach.

Eat inde sine die That he may go without delay—the words used to acquit or release a defendant from a criminal charge.

EAVESDROP To listen in on a private conversation.

EBRIETY Drunkenness; intoxication. The opposite state is sobriety.

ECCENTRICITY Peculiar conduct.

ECCHYMOSIS A bruise; a black-and-blue discoloration of the skin.

ECCLESIASTICAL COURTS A system of courts with jurisdiction over religious and spiritual matters.

ECCLESIASTICAL LAW The laws that govern the doctrines, discipline, and worship in established religions.

Ecdicus 1. A lawyer who represents a corporation. 2. A prosecutor.

ECHOLALIA The senseless repetition of certain words or phrases as a symptom of insanity.

ECONOMY 1. The cautious and careful handling of money. 2. The financial situation of a country or state.

E contraria On the contrary.

E converso Conversely.

ECUMENICAL Universal.

EDICT A new law proclaimed by the ruler of a country.

EDICTUM A law enacted by a Roman emperor without the approval of the senate.

EDMUNDS ACT A federal law against polygamy.

EEOC The abbreviation for the Equal Employment Opportunities Commission, a federal agency concerned with ending job discrimination.

EFFECT 1. (v.) To accomplish or bring about. 2. (n.) Result.

EFFIGY A dummy made to represent a real person.

EISNE The eldest son.

EISNETIA, OR EINETIA The share of a parent's estate that goes to the eldest son.

EJECT To throw out.

EJECTA A woman who is the victim of a rape.

EJECTMENT An action that arises when one person claims a right to possess certain real property that is possessed by another.

EJECTOR A person who throws another off a piece of property.

Ejusdem generis Of the same genre, or class.

ELECTION The act of choosing or making a choice.

ELECTOR A person with the right to vote.

ELECTROCUTION A method, used in some states to carry out a death sentence, in which electric current is passed through the body.

ELECTRONIC DEVICE An object that operates by electricity, usually used in reference to surveillance equipment used to eavesdrop or spy. Commonly a "bug."

ELEEMOSYNARY Charitable.

ELEMENT 1. An essential part or component (of a crime). 2. One of the forces of nature.

ELIGIBLE Qualified; fit.

ELINGUATION The cutting out of a criminal's tongue; a method of punishment still used in some countries.

ELISOR An acting sheriff, appointed when a sheriff has been accused of having a vested interest in some matter.

ELOPEMENT 1. Commonly, a secret flight of two unmarried people in order to get married without a parent's consent. 2. A wife's desertion of her husband in order to live with another man.

EMANCIPATION 1. Liberation; the setting free of someone who is controlled by another. 2. The release of a minor from the control of his parents.

EMANCIPATION PROCLAMATION President Lincoln's proclamation ending slavery in the United States, effective January 1, 1863.

EMBEZZLEMENT The appropriation of money or property by someone who has been lawfully entrusted with it. Example: A bank teller has a right to hold money for his bank, but he becomes an embezzler if he uses the money for himself.

EMBLEMENTS Crops that are growing.

EMBRACEOR A person who commits the crime of embracery.

EMBRACERY The crime of bribing or attempting to bribe a juror.

EMERGENCY A sudden, unexpected crisis.

EMIGRANT AGENT A person who hires laborers to work in another state.

EMINENT DOMAIN A right of the state to confiscate private property for public use, in return for just compensation to the owner of the property.

EMISSARY 1. A diplomat sent on a mission by his government. 2. A person sent on a mission by his employer.

EMOLUMENT, OR PERQUISITE 1) Gain from employment. 2) A private or public advantage obtained by a business executive or a political officeholder. For example, the use of a company car or airplane for entertaining clients. Popularly called "perk."

EMPIRICAL Based on observation, experiments, or experience.

EMPLOYEE Someone who works for another for a wage.

EMPLOYER Someone who hires another to work for a wage.

EMPOWER To grant authority.

Emptio Purchase.

Emptor A buyer.

Emptor emit quam minimo potest, venditor vendit quam maximo potest "A buyer purchases for the lowest price he can; a seller sells for the highest price he can."

En banc (Fr.) On the bench. All the judges who sit on the bench of a specific court.

EN ROUTE On the way (to a destination).

ENABLING STATUTES Laws that confer new powers.

ENACTING CLAUSE A part of a statute or written law declaring its enactment and identifying the legislature responsible for making the law.

ENCROACH The gradual and unlawful take-over of another's property rights.

ENCROACHMENT Use of the real property of another. Example: a part of a building that intrudes upon a street or a neighboring piece of property.

ENCUMBRANCE A right in real property or a claim against a piece of property, such as a mortgage. (Also incumbrance.)

ENDORSE See INDORSE.

ENDOWMENT A fund set up usually to benefit some public institution such as a school.

ENFORCE To require, urge, or compel.

ENJOIN To command, direct, or instruct with authority, usually to restrain or forbid some activity.

ENLIST 1. To join in a cause. 2. To join the military.

ENLIST AID To seek help.

ENROLL To register, or place on a roll.

ENSUE To follow.

ENTAIL An estate limited to specified heirs.

ENTICE Unlawfully to persuade or seduce.

ENTICEMENT Unlawful seduction.

ENTIRE Whole and undivided.

ENTIRETY Wholeness; completeness.

ENTITLE 1. To provide a basis or cause for a claim. 2. To give a right or title.

ENTITY A being.

ENTRAP To catch, trap, or snare.

ENTRAPMENT A defense used in a criminal action charging that police caused the defendant to commit a crime that he ordinarily would not have done.

ENTRY 1. The act of recording something in a ledger. 2. The act of going into a building.

ENTRY OF JUDGMENT A formal recording of a judicial decision in the official records by the court clerk.

ENUMERATED Specifically mentioned.

ENUMERATORS Census takers.

ENVIRONMENTAL IMPACT STATEMENT A written report outlining in detail the effect that a proposed real estate development would have on the surrounding area if completed.

ENVIRONMENTAL LAW A broad term for laws and legal actions intended to protect against hazards resulting from the exploitation of nature. Examples: laws limiting air pollution or protecting animal species.

ENVOY A diplomatic officer of lesser rank than an ambassador.

Eo nomine Under that name. Often used in reference to something that is known by more than one name.

EPA The abbreviation for the Environmental Protection Agency, a federal agency that enforces anti-pollution laws and acts as a watchdog on environmental questions.

E pluribus unum One out of many. The motto of the United States of America.

EQUAL PROTECTION OF THE LAW A constitutional provision (in the Fourteenth Amendment) designed to prevent the government from creating laws to justify treating people unequally.

EQUIP To outfit, supply, or furnish in preparation for some activity or event.

EQUITABLE ESTOPPEL A rule that allows a person who has acted in reliance on another's promise to seek a remedy in the courts should that promise be revoked or should affirmations be fraudulent.

EQUITY A form of justice based on what is fair and just, as opposed to strict adherence to the written law. Equity actions do not seek monetary amends but, rather, some form of action such as injunctions or specific performance of a contract.

EQUITY FOR REDEMPTION The right of a mortgagor to regain his property after he has failed to make payments and therefore lost the legal right to it.

ESCHEAT The state's acquisition of ownerless property, usually when a person dies without leaving heirs.

ESCROW Something (usually real property) that is withheld from the owner and entrusted to a third person until the owner fulfills an obligation owed to someone else. Today, rent payments may be held in escrow to force a landlord to make building repairs.

ESTATE An interest, right, or title to property.

ESTATE TAX A tax on property that is owned by a decedent at his death.

ESTOPPEL A doctrine of law that prevents a party from making a claim or a statement contrary to actions previously taken by the party or by the court. For example, if a person signs an agreement, that person might be prevented or "estopped," from later claiming that the agreement was wrong.

Et al. And others.

ETHICS Standards of conduct that are expected of people working within a given profession.

EUTHANASIA Causing death in order to end seemingly incurable suffering; mercy killing.

EVASION The act of purposely avoiding or eluding someone or something.

EVICTION The ejection or removal by process of law of a tenant from a landlord's property, usually for nonpayment of rent.

EVIDENCE Proof introduced at trial to persuade the court or jury of a position.

Ex contractu (An action arising) from a contract.

Ex delicto (An action arising) from a tort, or crime.

Ex dolo malo non oritur actio "A fraudulent actor cannot maintain an action."

Ex gratia (Done) as a favor.

Ex mero motu Voluntarily and without prompting.

Ex officio By the power of office.

Ex parte Dealing with one party only.

Ex post facto After the fact; (a law) that fixes a punishment for an act after it was committed.

EXCEPTION Something outside the normal rules and not confined by them.

EXCHANGE 1. The transfer of funds or goods from one party to another. 2. Barter.

EXCISE TAX A tax on the consumption of some commodity or on its retail sale.

EXCLUSIVE Dealing with a single subject only.

EXCLUSIONARY RULE A rule that evidence obtained illegally by the police will not be allowed in court.

EXCULPATORY Supporting the innocence of a defendant accused of a crime.

EXCULPATORY CLAUSE A provision or clause (in an agreement) that relieves one of the parties of any liability.

EXCUSABLE NONPERFORMANCE The failure to perform, as required by a contract, because such performance would be illegal.

EXCUSE A lawful reason for an act that would otherwise be unlawful.

EXECUTE 1. To complete, perform, or follow through with one's actions in regard to some legal matter. 2. To make; usually to sign and deliver, as a deed. 3. To collect a judgment debt.

EXECUTION The act of doing something to completion.

EXECUTOR A man appointed by a decedent to disperse the decedent's estate according to the decedent's wishes. (The comparable term for a woman is executrix.)

EXECUTORY In the process of being completed.

EXEMPLARY DAMAGES Punitive damages awarded for the purpose of setting an example for other offenders, particularly when the wrong was aggravated by violence or malice.

EXEMPTIONS Those things free from the burden of taxes or service.

EXHIBIT A piece of specific evidence accepted by the court and identified by a letter or number.

EXONERATE To prove one's innocence; to be freed from criminal liability.

EXONERATION Freedom from criminal charges; proof of innocence.

EXPENDITURE The spending of money.

EXPENSES Monetary obligations.

EXPERT WITNESS Someone who is recognized as being knowledgeable in some field of science or art, and whose experience is called on for the purpose of settling some courtroom dispute.

EXPRESSED STATEMENT A definite statement, either spoken or put into writing.

EXTORTION The crime of taking money by threat or force, as defined by various state statutes.

EXTRACTION OF CONFESSION A confession that is not given voluntarily but results from coercion.

EXTRADITION The giving up of a prisoner by a country or state for the purpose of having the prisoner stand trial for an offense committed in another country or state.

EXTRINSIC FRAUD An intentional act preventing an opposing party from seeking justice.

EYEWITNESS A person who testifies in court to some event he has seen with his own eyes.

◀ F ▶

FAA Abbreviation for the Federal Aviation Administration.

Facias What is done; what has been caused to happen.

Facio ut des A type of contract in which one party agrees to do something in return for money or wages.

Facio ut facias A type of contract in which one party agrees to do or refrain from doing something in return for the other party's promise to do or refrain from doing something.

FACSIMILE An exact copy, or replica.

FACT 1. That which has been done or has existed. 2. Events or things that have been proved by evidence. The jury decides if the proof is sufficient.

Facta sunt potentiora verbis "What is done is more powerful than what is said."

FACTOR An agent who possesses and seeks to sell goods belonging to a client, or principal.

FACTORS ACTS A common name for legislation making a principal responsible for any injurious acts committed by a factor who sells the principal's goods.

Factum a judice quod ad ejus officium non spectat, non ratum est "What a judge decides outside his office has no legal force."

Factum unius alteri noceri non debet "One's deeds should not bring harm to others."

FAILURE OF ISSUE Dying without leaving any children or other descendants.

FAILURE OF RECORD The inability or neglect on the part of a defendant, who has based his defense on a matter of record, to produce before the court the record on which his defense is based.

FAILURE OF TITLE The inability of a vendor to provide good title to something he has contracted to sell.

FAIR AND EQUITABLE A term that implies that an act was or is just and impartial, or that a price represents the true worth of an item.

FAIR MARKET VALUE The price that would be paid for something in a marketplace, that would be agreeable to both a willing buyer and a willing seller under normal conditions.

FAIR-TRADE ACTS Laws establishing minimum resale prices for goods sold by a retail storekeeper.

FAIR-TRADE LAWS State laws allowing manufacturers to fix the minimum price that a retailer may charge for the manufacturer's products.

FALSE Untrue or wrongful.

FALSE ARREST OR FALSE IMPRISONMENT An unlawful, unjustified confinement or restraint of a person. Example: detention of an innocent shopper by store guards who accuse him of shoplifting.

FALSE PRETENSES Untrue statements or misrepresentations made in order to obtain valuables belonging to another.

FALSIFY To alter something in order to fool someone.

Falsus in uno, falsus in omnibus "False in one thing, false in all."

FAMILY BIBLE A Bible in which are recorded births, deaths, and marriages of family members.

FAMILY-CAR DOCTRINE A principle in some jurisdictions holding the owner of a family car liable for injuries caused by its negligent operation by any family member.

FAMILY RELATIONS An area of the law that deals primarily in divorces, alimony, adoption, and other legal affairs that affect the family unit.

FAS Free alongside; delivery of goods to the means of shipment without paying freight costs or assuming liability for shipment.

Fasti Lawful. *Fasti dies* or *dies fast,* refers to legal business days in general, and during Roman times in particular it referred to days on which the Roman courts could administer justice.

FAULT The responsibility for a misdeed or for negligence.

FBI Abbreviation for Federal Bureau of Investigation.

FCC Abbreviation for Federal Communications Commission.

FDA Abbreviation for Food and Drug Administration.

FEASANCE An act, accomplishment, or performance.

FEASOR A person who does something.

FEDERAL DEPOSIT INSURANCE CORPORATION (FDIC) A federally owned company set up to insure the money that customers deposit in bank accounts.

FEDERAL HOUSING ACT (FHA) A federal act established to encourage people to buy houses that meet building codes.

FEDERAL OFFENSES Violations of federal statutes.

FEDERAL RESERVE ACT A federal act establishing privately owned federal reserve banks in order to furnish certain services required by commercial banks.

FEDERAL RESERVE BANK A privately owned bank that furnishes certain services exclusively to commercial banks.

FEE 1. A charge for services performed by government employees or professionals. 2. The ownership of land, or the land itself.

FEE SIMPLE An estate that is left to an heir without any restrictions by the owner of the estate.

FEE TAIL An estate that is left to an heir and a fixed line of future heirs by the owner of the estate.

Felo-de-se A person who is guilty of committing suicide; a suicide victim in a jurisdiction where killing oneself is a felony.

FELONIUS HOMICIDE The unjustified, inexcusable killing of a human being.

FELONY A serious, or high, crime.

FELONY MURDER A homicide committed during the course of a felonious crime. Example: A thief kills someone during a bank robbery, thus committing a felony murder even though he didn't intend to kill anyone.

FELONY-MURDER RULE In most jurisdictions, a homicide that is committed during the course of a serious crime is to be regarded as first-degree murder.

Femme covert (Fr.) A married female.

Femme sole (Fr.) An unmarried female.

FENCE 1. A person who buys stolen property to resell at a profit. 2. The buying of stolen property.

Ferae naturae Of nature; wild animals.

FEUD 1. In the Middle Ages, an inherited right to occupy and use the land of feudal estate. 2. A private, mutual hostility between two families or two branches of the same family.

FETICIDE The killing of an unborn child.

FETUS An unborn child.

Fiat justitia, ruat coelum "Let justice be done, even though the heavens fall."

FICTION An assumption, not based on fact, that is used by a court in support of the court's decision.

FICTITIOUS NAME A false name taken for the purpose of deceiving someone; an alias.

FIDUCIARY A person entrusted with the duty to act for the benefit of someone else. A high degree of care attaches to a person in this position. Examples: a trustee; a director of a corporation.

Fieri facias A court order commanding a sheriff to seize the property of a debtor in order to pay off a debt.

FIFTH AMENDMENT An amendment to the United States Constitution providing a person with the right not to say things that might incriminate him.

FIGHT Combat.

FILING The act of delivering some document to an officer of the courts, usually a clerk.

FILIBUSTER 1. One who wages unauthorized warfare against

a foreign country. 2. The practice of blocking legislation by introducing long speeches or irrelevant issues.

Filum A line or boundary, usually through a stream or road.

FINAL Conclusive; last.

FINANCE CHARGE The cost of a loan of money; interest.

FINAL SETTLEMENT The declaration by a judge in a probate proceeding that the administrator of an estate has finally completed his duties.

FINANCIAL STATEMENT A written report of what a person or a company owns, also stating what debts are owed.

FINDER A term for a person who discovers the lost property of another.

FINDER'S FEE A reward paid to a person who finds something that someone else wants.

FINDING OF FACT A fact that has been determined by the court.

FINE A punishment requiring the payment of money.

FIREBUG A criminal who starts fires; an arsonist or pyromaniac.

FIRM OFFER A written offer by a merchant to sell or buy something at a stated price within a period of time.

FIXTURE An article that is permanently attached to a piece of land or a building.

FLIMFLAM Trickery used to obtain another person's money.

FLOTSAM The debris of shipwrecks found floating on the water. (See JETSAM.)

FOB Abbreviation for *freight on board;* goods delivered to a form of transportation for shipment to a buyer by the seller and at the seller's expense. The seller's liability ends only when the goods are delivered to the buyer.

FORBEARANCE TO ACT Refraining from taking some action.

FORCED SALE A sale of real property, merchandise, or stock as ordered by a judge, usually to satisfy a debt.

Force majeure (Fr.) A superior, unyielding force.

FORCIBLE DETAINER The possession of a piece of real property by force or violence by a person not entitled to possess the property.

FORCIBLE ENTRY The taking of land or buildings through violence or threat of violence.

FORECLOSURE 1. The public sale of mortgaged property for the purpose of raising money to pay off the mortgage debt. 2. The taking of mortgaged property away from a property owner because he has failed to make payment.

FORENSIC Having to do with courts of law.

FORENSIC MEDICINE Medical knowledge that is valuable to the courts.

FORESEEABLE CONSEQUENCE The presumed result of an act.

FORFEITURE The loss of some privilege or property as a penalty for some error, offense, or nonperformance of a condition.

FORGE 1. To tamper with (an existing legal document) for wrongful purposes. 2. To make a legal-looking document intended to deceive someone into thinking that it is a lawful document; to counterfeit a document or signature.

FORGERY The making or altering of a document that, if genuine, would be valid for the purpose it was contrived for; the counterfeiting of an object such as a check with intent to defraud. False signature, alteration of the amount of a check, and misuse of a document are all forgery.

Forma dat esse Form proves existence. A thing with a physical shape or form is not imaginary; it exists.

FORMALITY An orderly method specified by law for the making of a legal document or a judicial proceeding in order to insure legitimacy.

FORMER JEOPARDY A plea that the defendant has been tried once, and cannot be tried again, for the same crime.

FORMS OF ACTION A term encompassing the many categories of legal actions to recover personal property, breach of contract, or injuries to person or property, as developed by the common law.

FORNICATION Sexual intercourse between unmarried persons, classed as a misdemeanor in some states.

FORTUITOUS Resulting from good (or bad) fortune or luck.

Forum non conveniens A doctrine that permits a court to decline to try a case if the dispute can be settled in another court, where it would be more convenient for litigants and witnesses.

FOUNDLING HOME A home for parentless children; an orphanage.

FRANCHISE 1. A special privilege conferred on an individual or a corporation by a government. 2. The privileged use of a trade name conferred by the owner of the trade name, usually for consideration. Example: Owners of fast-food restaurants often own a franchise from the parent company. 3. The right to vote.

FRANCHISED DEALER A merchant privileged to use the trade name of a corporation.

FRANKING 1. The practice of sending letters without having to pay postage. 2. Getting something free. An example would be the privilege of a congressman to mail letters without having to pay for postage stamps.

FRAUD The use of deceit to gain an unfair advantage over another, in order to secure something of value or deprive another of a right; any artifice used to deceive others.

FRAUDULENT CONVEYANCE The transfer of property with the intent to deceive a creditor; often used in bankruptcy proceedings.

FREEHOLD 1. The ownership of a piece of real property. 2. An estate.

FRISK A rapid search of the suspect to see if he is carrying a weapon.

Fructus industriales The fruits of industry; things that are brought about through labor and toil.

Fructus naturales The fruits of nature; things that result from the powers of nature.

Frustra probatur quod probatum non relevat "It is useless to prove what is not relevant."

FRUSTRATION A hindrance of some condition in a contract that cannot be attributed to either of the contracting parties and that makes performance of the contract impossible.

FUGITIVE A person who commits a crime, then leaves the state to avoid apprehension.

FULL-FAITH-AND-CREDIT CLAUSE A constitutional provision requiring every state to recognize the judicial rulings of other states to the same extent that those judgments are recognized in the home state.

FUNGIBLE GOODS Items identical in every way; for example, one sixty-watt light bulb of a specific quality is identical to every other sixty-watt light bulb of similar quality.

Furiosi nulla voluntas est A madman has no free will. An insane person cannot be held responsible for his conduct, since madness does not allow him to act according to his own free will.

FUTURE ESTATE OR INTEREST A person's stake in some piece of property that is not owned by the person but will be at some time in the future. Example: an interest in a house to begin at the death of someone now alive.

◀ G ▶

GALLOWS 1. A structure built for hanging criminals. 2. Commonly, any facility for executing criminals.

GAME OF CHANCE A contest or sport in which skill, talent, or practice are of no advantage to the participants.

GAOL Jail.

GAOLER Jailer.

GARNISH To attach or seize money or property to pay a debt.

GARNISHEE The person holding the money or property that someone seeks to attach.

GARNISHMENT A process by which a debt is collected to pay off another debt. Example: A garnishes money B owes to C in order to satisfy C's debt to A.

GENDARME A policeman in a country where the police are a branch of the military.

GENERAL ACCOUNTING OFFICE (GAO) An office that helps Congress audit and investigate federal programs.

GENERAL ASSIGNMENT The transfer of the property of a person in debt to a fiduciary who pays off the creditors.

GENERAL DENIAL A defendant's denial of all charges or complaints brought against him.

GERMANE Relevant or important.

GESTATION The time between conception and the birth of a child, usually nine months.

GIFT A voluntary transfer of ownership of something to someone else, without further consideration.

GIFT *causa mortis* A gift made because the donor's death is imminent; such a gift may be revoked if the donor doesn't die.

GIST The real meaning, point, or heart of some matter.

GOOD CAUSE A logical, necessary, or just reason for doing something; a legally sufficient reason.

GOOD FAITH A term used to denote one party's reliance on the complete honesty of another party in commercial dealings.

GOODWILL The reputation of a business and patronage of regular customers, acquired by doing business over a period of time.

GOVERNMENT *de facto* The government in power.

GOVERNMENT *de jure* The lawful government.

GRAND JURY A body of people selected according to law to investigate crimes and indict suspected persons when sufficient evidence has been discovered to warrant holding a suspected person for trial.

GRAND LARCENY A high degree of theft, determined by the value of the object stolen.

GRANT 1. To give or allow. 2. A gift or present, especially of land.

GRANTEE A person who receives a grant.

GRANTOR A person who grants something to another.

Gratis Free.

GRATUITOUS PROMISE An agreement, to do or refrain from doing something that is not supported by consideration.

GRATUITY A gift.

Gravamen The primary, essential part of any complaint or cause of action.

GROSS INCOME 1. The total earnings of a person or business. 2. For income tax purposes, all money coming in, from whatever source.

GROSS NEGLECT A high degree of neglect, determined variously by various jurisdictions.

GROSS NEGLIGENCE A high degree of negligence, determined variously by various jurisdictions. Negligence is considered gross when there is such a disregard for the rights of others that willfulness can be presumed.

GROSS WEIGHT The complete weight of something. Example: The gross weight of a truck would be the weight of the truck and the cargo it carries.

GROUND RENT Money paid for the use of land in accordance with a lease.

GUARANTOR A person who guarantees something.

GUARANTY, OR GUARANTEE 1. An agreement in which one party makes a promise to answer for the default of a debtor. 2. An implied or expressed agreement between a manufacturer and dealer and a purchaser to assure a product's integrity. 3. The act of assuming responsibility for performance.

GUARDIAN A person appointed by the court to care for and manage the affairs of someone who is considered unable to take care of his own affairs.

GUARDIAN *ad litem* A guardian appointed by the court to represent an infant and to defend him or her, or to bring an action in court in the infant's behalf.

GUEST STATUTE Laws that vary from state to state and that, in general, provide for a special standard of care due a passenger in an automobile by the owner or driver of the automobile.

GUILT The responsibility for a wrongdoing.

GUILTY A verdict returned by a jury when it finds that the defendant has committed a crime as charged.

◀ H ▶

Habeas corpus, WRIT OF A court order requiring a prisoner to be produced in court so that the legality of his detention can be looked into.

Habeas corpus ad prosequendum A writ that is issued to move a prisoner from one jurisdiction to another for prosecution in the jurisdiction where an event at issue occurred.

Habeas corpus ad testificandum A writ that enables a prisoner in jail to testify in court; literally, that you may have the body to testify.

Habendum The clause in a deed that describes the extent of ownership in the thing covered by the deed.

HABITATION The right of a person to live in the house of another.

HAMLET A small town or village.

HARD LABOR Punishment beyond imprisonment, usually in the form of arduous manual labor.

HARASS To repeatedly annoy, irritate, anger, worry, embarrass, torment, or plague.

HEARING A court proceeding in which evidence is brought before a judge to determine whether or not the accused person should be held for trial.

HEARSAY Statements made by a witness that are not based on personal knowledge or observation but are simply the repetition of what someone else has said. It is inadmissible in court, in most cases, because the original speaker of the words was not under oath.

HEARSAY RULE A rule that hearsay evidence is generally inadmissible under Uniform Rule of Evidence 63, except to show that *words* were spoken by someone; the content of the spoken words, however, is inadmissible.

HEIR 1. In civil law, anyone who inherits an estate and incurs the rights and obligations of the decedent. 2. In common law, anyone appointed by law to take over the estate of someone who dies without leaving a will.

HEREDITAMENTS A term for property and rights that can be inherited.

HEW The abbreviation for the Department of Health, Education, and Welfare.

HIGH SEAS The portion of the oceans that is not within the boundaries of any country.

HIGHWAYMAN A robber, or bandit, who holds up travelers.

Hoc In this.

Hoc anno This year.

HOLDER IN DUE COURSE Someone who, in good faith and for value, takes over a note that, to his knowledge, neither is overdue nor has been previously dishonored.

HOLDING 1. The decision of a court. 2. The decision of an appellate court agreeing with the decision of the lower court.

HOLDOVER A tenant who keeps possession of property, after his lease has expired, without the consent of the landlord.

HOME The dwelling place of a person or family.

HOMESTEAD The home and land owned by the head of a family and used as the family's residence; it is protected by law from forced sale by creditors.

HOMESTEAD ACT A law that allows private citizens to settle and claim ownership of public land after meeting certain requirements such as making certain improvements and setting up residence on the property.

HOMESTEAD EXEMPTION LAWS Laws that allow a homeowner to make his home and the property it sits on exempt from a forced sale in order to pay his debts.

HOMICIDE Any killing of one human being by another, whether accidentally or deliberately.

HORNBOOK A textbook containing the basic principles of an area of the law.

HOSTILE WITNESS A witness who dislikes the party who has called him to testify. A hostile witness can be cross-examined by the party that called him as if the opposition had called him.

HOUSE OF ILL FAME OR ILL REPUTE A house of prostitution; a brothel.

HUD The abbreviation for the Department of Housing and Urban Development.

HUE AND CRY A vocal solicitation for assistance while in pursuit of a suspected felon.

HUNG JURY A jury unable to decide on a verdict.

HUSBAND A married man.

HUSH MONEY A bribe given a witness to keep him from giving to the court information regarding some unlawful activity.

HYPOTHECATE To pledge (a thing) without delivering possession (of the thing) to the pledgee.

HYPOTHETICAL QUESTION A question based on assumed (not proved) facts, asked of an expert witness. Example: "Could a blowgun be accurate at one hundred yards?"

◀ I ▶

Ibid., OR *ibidem* In the same place. Commonly used in footnotes meaning that the information will be found on the same page in the same book as the previous footnote.

Ictus orbis A bodily injury in which the skin is not cut or broken; a bruise or a swelling.

Id certum est quod certum reddi potest "It is certain only when it is made certain"; a fact is not a fact until it is proved.

Idem est non probari et non esse "What is unproved and what does not exist are the same."

Idem est scire aut scire debere aut potuisse "To be required to know, or to be able to know, is the same as to know."

IDENTICAL Exactly alike; the same.

IDENTIFICATION Proof of a person's identity.

Identitas vera colligitur ex multitudine signorum "True identity can be discovered by a number of signs."

IDIOCY The condition of possessing an unsound mind as a result of a congenital mental defect.

IDIOT The possessor of an unsound mind since birth (presumed never able to recover).

Id possumus quod de jure possumus "We may do only what is allowed by the law."

Ignis judicum Trial by fire.

IGNOMINY Disgrace; dishonor.

IGNORANCE The condition of not knowing about some previous or existing thing.

Ignorantia juris quod quisque tenetur scire, neminem excusat "Ignorance of a law that everyone is supposed to know is no excuse."

Ignorantia legis neminem excusat "Ignorance of the law is no excuse."

ILL FAME A bad reputation.

ILLEGAL Contrary to, or in violation of, the law.

ILLEGAL CONTRACT A contract made for unlawful purposes, such as to commit a crime.

ILLEGALITY A word used in reference to any act that is contrary to the law.

ILLEGITIMATE CHILD A child born of parents who are not married to each other at the time of the child's birth (or, in some cases, at the time of its conception).

ILLICIT Prohibited; not allowed by law.

ILLICIT COHABITATION Members of opposite sexes living together without being married.

ILLITERATE Unable to read and write.

ILLUSORY Deceiving, unreal.

ILLUSORY PROMISE A false and deceptive statement that appears to be a promise but is not. An example would be a "contract" that in fact promises nothing in return for the other party's money.

IMMATERIAL Trivial; without purpose or relevance to the issue at hand.

IMMINENT DANGER Danger that is so immediate that help cannot be called, making it necessary to meet the danger.

IMMORAL CONDUCT A lawyer's willful conduct of such a wrongful nature that his disbarment is called for.

IMMORAL CONSIDERATION An immoral inducement to enter into a contract.

IMMOVABLES Objects that cannot be moved or transported in a normal manner, such as a house or a piece of land.

IMMUNITY Freedom from some punishment, or exemption from some duty. An offer of immunity can be used to induce a witness to give up his Fifth Amendment rights.

IMPAIR 1. To make worse. 2. To lessen in effectiveness.

IMPARLANCE Literally "talk together." The time granted to the defendant for pleading.

IMPARTIALITY The fair and equal treatment of all parties.

IMPEACHMENT 1. The accusing and calling down of a public official for committing a wrongful act or wrongful acts while in office. 2. An attack on the credibility of a witness.

IMPEDIMENT Something that prevents a party from making a lawful contract. Example: insanity.

Imperitia A lack of skill.

Imperitia culpae adnumeratur "A professional's lack of skill in his work will be his responsibility."

IMPLEAD To prosecute or to lawfully bring a lawsuit against someone in a court of law.

IMPLIED Not expressed in writing or in words, but gathered from the facts.

IMPLIED CONDITION A condition not expressed by words or writing but considered to be tacitly assumed by the parties.

IMPLIED CONTRACT A contract arising out of the conduct of the parties involved, rather than out of words or writing.

IMPLIED WARRANTY 1. A warranty for fitness that is applicable to all goods sold unless it is expressly stated that the goods are sold "as is." 2. Any warranty inferred by the nature of a transaction. Example: In renting an apartment, there is an implied warranty that the place will be fit to live in.

IMPOSSIBILITY Something contrary to nature. Most often used in reference to contracts in which, for some reason, performance is no longer possible and the parties will not be held to the contract.

Impossibilum nulla obligatio est "There is no obligation to something that is impossible."

IMPOTENCE The inability of males to perform the sexual act.

Impotentia excusat legem "Impossibility is an excuse for not doing what the law requires."

IMPOUND To place something in custody until a legal question concerning it is decided.

IMPRISONMENT The physical confinement of a person.

IMPROVEMENTS Things that increase the value of usefulness of land or buildings.

IMPUNITY Protection from legal prosecution or punishment.

IMPUTABILITY The doctrine of holding a person responsible for that which he had no knowledge of but should have had knowledge of.

IMPUTE To attribute or charge someone with a legal responsibility.

IMPUTED NEGLIGENCE A condition whereby a person is held legally responsible for the negligence of another. Example: A parent is responsible for the negligence of a child.

In adversum 1. Against an adversary. 2. Against an unwilling party.

In alio loco In another place.

IN CAHOOTS Two or more parties acting in partnership, or for a mutual cause, are said to be acting in cahoots.

INCEST Sexual intercourse between persons closely related by blood, a crime often defined in state statutes.

INCHOATE Partial or incomplete; usually in reference to an unrecorded document.

INCOME TAX A tax on profits, wages, etc.

INCOMPATIBILITY The condition of two or more persons or things that cannot exist together. In many states this is grounds for separation or divorce.

INCOMPETENCE The inability to perform a required duty.

INCOMPETENT A person who is unable to manage his own affairs.

INCORPORATION The act of making a corporation.

INCORRIGIBILITY Not able to be corrected or reformed. Hardened criminals are said to be incorrigible.

In criminalibus, probationes debent esse luce clariores "In criminal cases, proof should be as clear as daylight."

INDECENT EXPOSURE A statutory offense consisting of the lewd exhibition of the private parts of the body in a public place.

INDEFINITENESS Vagueness, or lack of certainty.

In delicto At fault.

INDEMNIFY 1. To insure another against particular losses. 2. To make good.

INDEMNITY A contract to insure a person against a specific loss; security to make a person whole if he suffers some loss.

INDENTURE 1. A written instrument that is torn in half, each half being identical to the other and held by each party to the instrument. 2. A deed providing for reciprocal grants and obligations.

INDEPENDENT CONTRACTOR A person who contracts to work on his own for another and who is not under the other's control, as an employee is, as to the details of the work.

INDETERMINATE SENTENCE A prison sentence of an indefinite period of time.

INDICIA Indications of the probability of a given fact.

INDICT To accuse someone of having committed a crime, especially an accusation in writing by a grand jury.

INDICTEE A person who is being indicted.

INDICTOR The person who accuses someone of having committed a crime.

INDICTMENT A written formal accusation that charges a person with having committed a crime, usually presented by a grand jury.

INDIGENCE Poverty.

INDIGNITY Insult or unworthy treatment.

INDORSE 1. To sign a piece of paper. 2. To recommend something, usually in return for consideration.

INDORSEE A person who receives an indorsed piece of paper.

INDORSEMENT The signature on a negotiable instrument that

allows the paper, and what it represents, to be transferred to another.

INDORSER A person who signs a negotiable instrument.

In dubio In doubt.

In dubio, sequendum quod tutius est "When in doubt, the safest course is the best."

INDUCE To cause something to happen.

INDUCEMENT A promise or gift made to cause another to do something.

INDUCTION Steps taken for entry into military service.

INELIGIBLE Not qualified; out of the running.

INESCAPABLE PERIL A dangerous situation that is completely unavoidable.

In esse In existence.

In facto In fact.

INFAMOUS Wicked, evil, heinous.

INFAMY A loss of certain rights or privileges resulting from conviction for committing a crime punishable by prison.

INFANCY The legal condition or state of an infant.

INFANT A legal minor.

INFANTICIDE The crime of murdering a child.

INFERENCE Something that is probably true because it logically follows other facts.

In flagrante delicto In the commission of a crime.

INFORMANT A person who provided information regarding criminal activity.

INFORMATION 1. Knowledge or intelligence. 2. A formal, written accusation made by a district attorney, sometimes to induce a grand jury to make an indictment.

INFORMER A person who provides the police with the information about criminals.

Infra Under, below; the opposite of *supra.*

Infra aetatem Under age; minor.

Infra furorem During madness.

Infra jurisdictionem Under jurisdiction.

INFRACTION A breaking or violation of a law, contract, obligation, or duty.

INFRINGEMENT An encroachment on property or the unauthorized use of something that belongs to another, especially a copyright, patent, or trademark.

INFRINGER A person who uses something, especially a patent, copyright, or trademark, belonging to another, without the authority to do so.

INGRESS AND EGRESS Entry and exit. Refers to a lessee's right to enter and leave the property being leased.

INHERITANCE Real or personal property that is left to an heir upon the death of the owner; strictly, property received on an ancestor's death.

In initio Initially; at the beginning. Describes the opening stages of a lawsuit.

In invitum Describes legal proceedings against an unwilling party, such as a trial in which the defendant has no desire to appear before the court and must be forced against his will to stand trial.

INJUNCTION An order by a judge commanding that a person perform or refrain from performing certain acts. Example: A court order forbidding the construction of a building until a zoning law is clarified.

INJURED PARTY A person or group of persons that have sustained damage because of the actions of another.

Injuria absque damno A wrongdoing that causes no loss or damages, so it cannot be used as grounds for a lawsuit.

Injuria non excusat injuriam "One wrong will not excuse another."

Injuria non praesumitur "An injury is not presumed"; an injury must first be proved in court before damages can be awarded.

INJURIOUS FALSEHOOD A lie that injures or damages a person.

INJURY Any wrong that does harm to another in his person, reputation, rights, or property.

In limine At the beginning.

INMATE 1. A person who lives in another person's home. 2. A person who is confined in a jail or prison.

INNKEEPER Anyone who, in the course of business, provides lodging to another.

In odium spoliatoris omnia praesumuntur "One who destroys evidence may be presumed to be guilty."

In pari delicto "Equally guilty." When opposing parties in a lawsuit are declared *in pari delicto,* the courts will aid neither side.

In personam (A legal action) against a person.

INQUEST 1. A hearing held to determine the circumstances of a suspicious death. 2. A body of men appointed to inquire into any matter.

In re Describes a judicial inquiry into a legal matter in which there is no plaintiff or defendant but rather a thing needing to be settled, such as an estate in probate.

In rem Describes a legal action against a thing itself, rather than its owner. An example would be a creditor's lawsuit to attach the property of a debtor as opposed to a lawsuit against the *debtor* personally to require payment of the debt.

INSANITY Madness; a mental disorder that prevents a person from distinguishing between right and wrong, or from seeing the consequences of his acts.

INSOLVENCY Inability of a person to pay his debts.

INSOLVENT A person without the means to pay his debts.

In specie In a specified way, or manner.

INSTALLMENT CONTRACT An agreement to pay for or deliver goods in separate payments, or lots.

In statu quo Being in the same situation, or state.

INSTRUMENT A formal legal document such as a deed or a bond.

INSUFFICIENCY The fault of an answer that does not respond specifically to the charges made in a bill or to the question asked.

INSURABLE INTEREST Ownership of or an interest in a piece of property or in the life of another (and of course in one's own life) which entitles the owner or interested party to obtain insurance against damage, loss, or death. For example, because he risks losing his investment in the event of a fire, a homeowner has an insurable interest in his home.

INSURANCE A contract that provides for protection against a possible loss from specified perils in exchange for payment.

INSURED A person or thing protected by insurance.

INSURER A company engaged in the business of providing insurance.

INTANGIBLES Things having no physical being or determinable value.

INTEGRATED AGREEMENT A final agreement on the wording of a proposed contract by the parties concerned with the agreement. An agreement is "integrated" when the parties are mutually satisfied with the terms of the contract.

INTENT The mental plan to do an act.

Inter alia Among other things.

Inter arma silent leges "In wartime, the laws are silent."

Inter sese OR *Inter se* Among themselves.

INTEREST 1. Ownership of something. 2. A share in something. 3. Money paid or received for the use of something, generally money.

INTERLOCUTORY DECREE A temporary order or decree made by a judge during the course of a trial.

INTERPLEADER A procedure whereby two or more parties having a claim to the property of another party can be forced to join in a single lawsuit.

INTERPRETATION The true meaning of some document.

INTERROGATORIES A written list of questions asked by one of the parties in a trial, of the other party or of a witness.

INTESTATE Dying without leaving a valid will.

INTERVENOR A person who has some interest in the outcome of a lawsuit and is allowed by the court to join the original parties to the suit in order to protect his interests.

INTERVENTION A proceeding allowing a third party (intervenor) to join the original parties to a lawsuit.

In toto Entirely.

INTOXICATION The state of a person who is drunk, drugged, or poisoned.

INTRAFAMILY TORT ACTION A lawsuit by one or more members of a family against another member of the family for damages arising out of a tort. There is often the danger of collusion in such suits.

INVENTORY An itemized list of property giving the quantity and value of each item.

INVITEE A person who is invited upon the land or premises of another. Examples: house guests, theater patrons.

INVOLUNTARY BANKRUPTCY Bankruptcy arising from a petition by creditors contrary to the wishes of the debtor.

INVOLUNTARY INTOXICATION 1. The state of being drunk, drugged or poisoned against one's will or unknowingly. 2. A defense against criminal charges for crimes committed while in such a condition.

INVOLUNTARY MANSLAUGHTER The killing of another human being by a person in the process of committing an illegal act not amounting to a felony or a lawful act that improperly causes death.

Ipso facto By that same fact.

Ire ad largum To go free.

IRRESISTIBLE IMPULSE An impulse (to commit a crime) that arises from a mental defect or insanity.

ISSUE 1. (n.) A dispute that is taken to court. 2. (n.) Descendants from a common ancestor. 3. (v.) To send out.

ISSUE IN FACT A dispute over the facts of a case rather than a dispute over the law applicable to the case.

ISSUE IN LAW A dispute over how the law applies to a case in court.

ITINERANT A traveler; a vagabond.

◀ J ▶

JAIL A place where prisoners are kept isolated from society.

JANE DOE A fictitious name generally used for the purpose of identifying temporarily the corpse of a woman whose true identity is unknown. The name is also used to refer to a woman in a hypothetical situation.

JEDBURGH JUSTICE Lynch law; the hanging of a prisoner without the benefit of a trial. The term comes from a Scottish border town where cattle thieves were traditionally hung on the spot without a trial.

JEOPARDY Risk, danger, peril; the perilous position of someone who stands trial. Once a trial has started, a defendant cannot be tried again for the same offense unless a witness, judge, or juror becomes ill or dies.

JETSAM Goods thrown overboard from a ship and washed up on shore. (See FLOTSAM.)

JETTISON To throw (goods) overboard, especially to lighten a ship or airplane in distress.

JOBBER A person in the business of buying and selling for others; a wholesaler.

JOHN DOE A fictitious name generally used for the purpose of identifying temporarily the corpse of a man whose identity is unknown. The name is also used to refer to a man in a hypothetical situation.

JOHN DOE WARRANT A warrant or order for the arrest of someone whose true identity is not yet known.

JOINDER OF CLAIMS The consolidation of two or more claims to be dealt with in a single action.

JOINT 1. Bound together. 2. (Two or more parties) affiliated by a sharing of liability or credit.

JOINT DEBTOR Two or more persons bound together by a common debt.

JOINT ENTERPRISE Two or more persons bound together by a common undertaking; partners in a specific endeavor.

JOINTLY In union; together.

JOINT TENANCY The condition of a piece of real property in which a lawful interest is held by more than one person.

JOY RIDING The taking and using of an automobile without the consent of the owner.

JUDGE ADVOCATE GENERAL'S CORPS Military units concerned with the legal affairs of the Army, Navy, Air Force, and Marines.

JUDGE *pro tem.* OR *pro tempore* A judge appointed for a specific period of time.

JUDGMENT The decision of the court regarding a case brought before it.

JUDGMENT CREDITOR Someone who has a judgment allowing him to attach the property of a party owing him money.

JUDGMENT DEBTOR A debtor whose property can be attached by creditors.

JUDGMENT *in personam* A judgment upon a single person, as opposed to judgment upon a thing or some matter.

JUDGMENT *in rem* A judgment upon a thing or some matter as opposed to a judgment against a person.

JUDGMENT NOTE A promissory note that authorizes a representative to appear in court in the place of the debtor to confess to the sum owed in the event the debtor defaults.

JUDGMENT OF CONVICTION The punishment to which a convicted criminal is sentenced, as recorded by the court's clerk.

Judicandum est legibus, non exemplis "Judgment is from law, not precedent."

Judice non tenentur exprimere causam sententiae suae "Judges should not be required to explain the reasoning of their judgment."

Judicia posteriora sunt in lege fortiora "The later decisions are the stronger." Recent court decisions carry more weight than decisions made a long time ago.

JUDICIAL Under the authority of a judge.

JUDICIAL NOTICE The acceptance by a court of certain facts without requiring evidence. Such facts could be historical data or state laws.

JUDICIARY ACT OF 1789 The act of Congress organizing the federal court system.

Judicis est jus dicere non dare "It is for the judge to declare the law, not to make it."

Judicis est judicare secundum allegata et probata "It's a judge's duty to decide a case according to the facts and allegations."

Juncta juvant "Union is strength."

Junta An administrative body.

Jura publica anteferenda privatis "Public rights take preference over private rights."

Jurat The date, time, place, and witness to the swearing of an affidavit, usually found at the bottom of a document.

JURATION The swearing of an oath.

Jure uxoris By the right of a wife.

JURIDICAL Having to do with justice.

JURIDICAL DAYS The days on which cases are heard; the days when court is held.

Juris Of, or pertaining to, law.

JURISDICTION The legal authority to hear and try a case. Jurisdiction entails authority over the person or thing being tried, and competence to deal the type of action brought.

Juris Doctor (J.D.) Doctor of law. An academic degree granted by most law schools.

JURIST A judge, or a retired judge, especially one who is recognized as an expert in some area of law.

JURY A number of citizens sworn by the court to determine the facts of a case.

JURY BOX The place where a jury sits.

JURY INSTRUCTIONS A judge's explanation to the jury of the law applicable to the case.

JURY WHEEL A drum or hopper from which the names of jurors are drawn.

Jus abutendi The right to abuse. Meaning complete ownership of something, including the right to abuse the thing owned.

Jus civitatus The rights of a citizen.

Jus in re The complete right to something.

Jus mariti The right of a husband. Usually in reference to his acquiring his wife's estate through marriage.

Jus naturae The law of nature.

Jus publicum privatorum pactis mutari non potest "The right of the public cannot be altered (or destroyed) by private agreements."

Jus tertii The right of a third party.

Jus utendi The right to use property but not to destroy it.

JUSTICE OF THE PEACE A lower judicial officer charged with specific powers such as performing weddings and issuing warrants.

JUSTICIABLE Accountable to a judge; decribing those matters that must be decided in court.

JUSTIFIABLE HOMICIDE The killing of a human being in self-defense, in order to prevent a felony or for some other reason allowed by law.

JUSTIFICATION An acceptable reason for the defendant's actions.

JUVENILE COURT A court that hears cases pertaining to delinquent or neglected children.

JUVENILE DELINQUENT A minor who has committed an act that would be a crime if committed by an adult.

◀ K ▶

KANGAROO COURT A court where the outcome of the trial has been decided before the case is heard.

KEEP 1. To continue. 2. To take care of or manage a business. 3. To feed and take care of an animal. 4. To possess. 5. (n.) A tower in a castle that serves as a last line of defense should the castle be overrun by an enemy.

KEEPING A DISORDERLY HOUSE The offense of running a house of prostitution.

KEPT WOMAN A woman who allows herself to be possessed by a man, in return for a higher life-style.

KICKBACK Money or valuables used to bribe a public or corporate officer for doing a favor, especially in awarding a profitable contract to one company over others.

KIDNAPING The unlawful seizure and carrying away of a person against his will; unlawful secret detention.

KIN A person or persons related by blood.

KING'S BENCH The highest court in England. When a queen is the ruling monarch, the court is called the Queen's Bench.

KITING The practice of writing a check for more than the amount in a checking account, then depositing enough money into the checking account to cover the check.

KLEPTOMANIA A mental illness that causes an irresistible urge to steal anything, even though the thief may have no use for the item.

KNOWINGLY Intentionally and willfully.

KNOWLEDGE The mental awareness of fact or truth.

◂ L ▸

LACHES A party's unreasonable delay in following a legal remedy, with the result that the condition of the parties or property affected by the remedy might change; undue delay in asserting a claim.

LAME DUCK 1. A politician, still serving in office after defeat at the polls, before his elected successor takes over. 2. A person who buys more stock than he can pay for.

LAND GRANT A gift of land, usually by a government.

LANDLORD A person who leases or rents land or buildings to another.

LANDRUM-GRIFFIN ACT A federal law regulating the internal affairs of labor unions.

LAPSE 1. (v.) To expire or terminate, especially in regard to a right or privilege. 2. (n.) The failure of a testamentary gift.

LARCENY The unlawful taking and removing of another's possessions with the intent of depriving their rightful owner of them.

LASCIVIOUS Lustful, immoral, obscene.

LAST CLEAR CHANCE A doctrine adopted by some states whereby a defendant may be liable for injuries caused by the contributory negligence of the plaintiff if the defendant failed to exercise ordinary care at a time when he could have prevented the injury from occurring.

LATENT Hidden.

LATENT DEFECT A defect, or flaw, that cannot be discovered by casual observation.

LAW 1. A method for settling disputes and holding people responsible for their conduct within society. 2. A statute, or legislative enactment.

LAW MERCHANT A set of laws, based on fairness, governing transactions between merchants in medieval England and Europe. The law merchant has become the basis for today's commercial laws.

LAWSUIT A legal proceeding in a court of law.

LAWS OF OLÉRON An ancient maritime code from which many modern maritime laws descend.

Le salut du peuple est la suprême loi (Fr.) "The safety of the people is the supreme law."

LEADING CASE A court case often used as a precedent for later cases dealing with the same issues.

LEADING QUESTION A question worded in such a way that the lawyer asking the question can control the answer given by a witness.

LEASE The temporary transfer of rights (most often in real property) to another for a predetermined time at an agreed-upon price.

LEASEHOLD Land and buildings that are leased.

LEDGER A book in which a written record of a business's accounts are kept.

LEGACY An inheritance; a gift of property by a will.

LEGAL In agreement with the law.

LEGAL CAP Oversized paper commonly used by lawyers.

LEGAL FICTION An assumption not based on reality, used by a court to justify its decision.

LEGAL TENDER Paper or coins deemed sufficient by law for the payment of debts.

LEGATEE A person who receives a legacy.

Legem enim contractus dat "A contract creates a law"; a contract should be regarded as law by the people who are parties to it.

Leges posteriores priores contrarias abrogant "Recent laws overrule earlier contrary laws."

LEGITIM Under the common law, a portion of a parent's estate that was passed on to the children.

Legum Doctor (LL.D.) Doctor of Laws. An advanced academic degree in law.

LESSEE A person who possesses the right to property belonging to another by virtue of a lease.

LESSOR A person who leases a right to property from another.

LET To lease some form of real property.

LETTER OF CREDIT A written request to advance credit or money to a third party, which guarantees to repay the creditor.

LETTER OF MARQUE A commission granted by the government to privately owned ships to arm themselves and attack the ships of enemy countries during wartime.

LETTER OF SAFE CONDUCT A passport, granted by an enemy, that permits safe travel across enemy territory.

LETTERS TESTAMENTARY A written instrument issued by a court authorizing and empowering a person named an executor in a will to act in that capacity.

LEVITICAL DEGREES Degrees of kinship, within which persons are prohibited from marrying each other.

LEVY 1. To raise, assess, or collect; commonly refers to taxes. 2. To obtain money (to repay a debt) by seizing and selling the debtor's property. Usually done by a sheriff.

LEWD HOUSE A hotel often patronized by prostitutes with the knowledge of the hotel management.

Lex communis The common law.

Lex contractus The law of contracts; contract law.

Lex domicilii The laws of one's homeland.

Lex est dictamen rationis "Law is dictated by reason."

Lex fori The law of the country or state where a case is to be decided.

Lex loci The law of the country or state where a contract is made.

Lex mercatoria The law of merchants; business law.

Lex neminem cogit ad vana seu inutilia peragenda "The law does not force people to do useless things."

Lex non curat de minimis "The law is not concerned with trivial matters."

Lex non scripta The unwritten law. A term used in reference to customs commonly accepted as law even though no court recogizes them as such. An example is the belief that killing one's wife's lover is legal.

Lex reprobat moram "The law frowns on delays."

Lex scripta The written law; statutory law.

Lex semper dabit remedium "The law always provides a remedy."

Lex succurrit minoribus "The law will help children."

Lex terrae The law of the land.

LIBEL 1. Published writing (or pictures) that degrade and defame a person. 2. An admiralty proceeding, usually involving the seizure of a ship.

Liber homo A free man.

Libera batella The right to fish.

Liberum maritagium A dowry of land given to a bride and groom.

LICENSE 1. A document or certificate giving its possessor the permission to do something that would be illegal otherwise. 2. Permission for certain acts on another's land. This permission may be revoked at any time.

LICENSEE 1. A person who possesses a license. 2. A person who is permitted upon the property of another but who has no interest in the land.

LICENSOR A person with the authority to issue licenses.

LIEN A claim upon, or a right to retain possession of, property of another as security for some debt owed by the person to whom the property belongs.

LIFE ESTATE, OR LIFE TENANCY An interest in property that lasts for the life of the holder (or some other party by whose life the estate or tenancy is measured).

LIFE TABLES Statistical charts, published by the Department of Health, Education, and Welfare, stating how long people of various ages are expected to live, on the average.

LIFE TENANT A person who possesses a life estate.

Ligula A copy of a deed or court record.

LIMITATION A restriction.

LIMITED LIABILITY In corporations or limited partnerships, the risk of loss measured by the amount of investment.

LIMITED PARTNERSHIP An unincorporated alliance that restricts the liability of certain parties to the amounts they have invested.

LINDBERGH LAW A popular name for a federal law making kidnaping a capital offense.

LIQUIDATE To settle or adjust.

LIQUIDATED DAMAGES An amount of money, agreed on in advance and expressed in a contract, that one party agrees to pay should the contract be breached.

Lis pendens A lawsuit that is not yet decided or a notice of pending litigation involving certain property that puts potential buyers on the alert.

LITIGANT A person who is a party to a lawsuit.

LITIGATION 1. A contest. 2. A lawsuit to enforce some right.

LITIGATION EXPENSE The cost of maintaining a lawsuit, including lawyers' fees, court fees, and miscellaneous expenses.

LITTORAL RIGHTS Those rights associated with owning property on the shores of the seas or large lakes. (See RIPARIAN RIGHTS.)

LIVING SEPARATE AND APART The condition of a husband and wife who cease to live in the same household.

LOAN 1. The lending of something. 2. To supply a sum of money in exchange for an agreement to repay the sum plus interest.

LOCATION A letting for rent or hire.

LOCKOUT The practice of keeping employees out of their place of work in order to obtain labor agreements favorable to the employer.

Locus contractus The place where a contract was entered into.

Locus delicti The place where a tort, or wrongful act, was performed.

Locus in quo The place where; the location in which.

Locus poenitentiae An opportunity to withdraw from an act or contract.

Locus sigilli The place on a document where a seal is affixed; often abbreviated to L.S.

LONG-ARM STATUTE Various legislative acts enabling a court to have jurisdiction over someone in another state who is named as a defendant in a local action.

LOST PROPERTY Property that by misfortune has left the immediate possession of the owner, who does not know where it is or how to recover it.

LUMP-SUM ALIMONY The entire amount of alimony paid in one payment.

LYDFORD LAW The hanging of criminals without benefit of a fair trial; lynch law.

M

M'NAGHTEN RULE A test used in various jurisdictions for determining whether or not a defendant accused of murder is criminally responsible. Basically, if the defendant possessed an understanding of what he was doing, and that what he was doing was against the law, he is held responsible; if not, he is not held responsible.

MAGISTRATE A judge with limited powers.

MAGNA CARTA A document signed by the King of England in 1215 granting rights and privileges to English citizens.

Magna culpa Gross negligence.

MAINTAIN To support, defend, take care of, or carry on.

MAINTENANCE 1. The act of supporting, defending, taking care of, or carrying on. 2. The act of helping to carry on an action in which one has no lawful interest.

MAJORITY Full age; the age at which a person is deemed by law to be old enough to manage his own affairs.

Mala fide In bad faith.

MALFEASANCE An unlawful act, usually in reference to illegal acts committed by a public official.

MALICE The state of mind associated with the performance of an unjustified, illegal act that the actor knows will result in damage or injury.

MALICIOUS MISCHIEF The unlawful and intentional destruction or vandalism of someone's property.

MALICIOUS PROSECUTION An action brought for the purpose of injuring another, and without probable cause. If the action ends in favor of the person prosecuted, malicious prosecution is in turn actionable.

MALPRACTICE A term for unprofessional conduct, usually by a doctor or a lawyer.

Malum in se Wrongful in itself; against nature or morality.

Malum prohibitum Wrongful as a result of some statute or code; an offense against public policy.

MANAGER A person whose job is to run a business.

Mandamus A writ or order issued by a high court and commanding a public official or governmental branch to do something.

MANDATE A judicial order that either commands or authorizes some kind of action.

MANN ACT A federal law forbidding the transportation of women across state lines for immoral purposes.

MANSLAUGHTER The unlawful killing of another with malice or intention to do so.

MARGIN 1. A boundary. 2. A deposit paid to a stockbroker for a purchase of stock.

MARITAL BREAKDOWN A term implying some kind of disintegration of a marriage.

MARITAL MISCONDUCT Conduct by a spouse that is harmful or detrimental to the marriage.

MARITAL OBLIGATIONS The responsibilities and duties owed to one spouse by another.

MARITIME LAW An area of the law concerning ships, sailors, and ocean commerce.

MARKETABLE TITLE A clear title to a piece of land; absolute ownership of land.

MARRIAGE A state or condition whereby a man and a woman are united by law for a variety of reasons.

MARRIAGE LICENSE A legal permit to marry, issued by a public authority.

MARSHAL A federal court officer.

MARTIAL LAW Military government; control of civilians by the military, usually in time of war or civil turmoil.

MASTER In modern terms, an employer.

MATERIAL FACT A piece of information that it is necessary to know in order to decide a case or enter into a contract.

MATERIAL ISSUE The real issue being disputed in a court case.

MATERIAL WITNESS The only person who can provide a unique and important piece of testimony at a trial.

MATTER OF FACT A question that is answered by the testimony given by witnesses.

MATTER OF LAW An issue that is decided by applying existing laws to the facts presented in court.

MATTER OF RECORD Something that can be proved by checking an official record.

MATURITY 1. A state of full development. 2. The date when a promissory note becomes due.

MAXIM A general statement about something.

MAYHEM The intentional infliction of a serious wound that disfigures another or deprives him of some bodily member.

MECHANIC'S LIEN A legal claim entitling a workman to hold or secure property worked on until his charges are paid.

MEDIATION The practice of settling a dispute or argument by an unbiased third party, or mediator.

MEDIATOR An unbiased third party who attempts to settle an argument or dispute between two parties.

MEDICAL AID Services offered by a medical doctor to someone in need of treatment.

MEETING OF MINDS A mutual understanding, about the purpose of a contract, between the parties entering the contract.

MEMORANDUM 1. A brief, submitted to a judge, in which an attorney cites previous cases that support his client's position. 2. An interoffice communication regarding the law as it has been applied to specific problems.

Mens rea The criminal intent or criminal mental state of a person at the time he commits a crime.

MENTAL ANGUISH The emotional suffering of an injured party (humiliation, grief, anxiety or other distress), as opposed to physical pain.

MENTAL CRUELTY Habitual behavior indicating hatred of a married person for his or her spouse.

MENTAL DEFECT 1. Incompetence. 2. A mental disorder that would disqualify a person from serving as a juror.

MENTAL DISEASE Generally, any disease of the mind.

MERCANTILE Having to do with trade and commerce.

MERCHANTABLE GOODS Goods that can be sold.

MERCY KILLING Homicide committed for the sole purpose of ending the misery of a suffering person who is beyond hope of recovery.

MERETRICIOUS RELATIONSHIP 1. A legally void marriage that is continued. 2. A relationship for the purpose of unlawful sexual intercourse.

MERGER 1. The joining of two or more things, often referring to the absorption of a smaller company by a larger company. 2. The joining of two estates in land, usually resulting in complete ownership by one party.

MERITS The important issues decided in a lawsuit; the real reason for bringing a dispute into court.

MESNE Intermediate; middle.

MEXICAN DIVORCE The dissolution of a marriage according to the legal process of Mexico.

MILITARY LAW An area of the law that governs military personnel.

Minatur innocentibus qui parcit nocentibus "He who spares the guilty threatens the innocent."

MINERAL RIGHTS The ownership of minerals in a specific piece of land, plus the right to remove those minerals with or without the consent of the landowner.

MINIMUM WAGE The lowest wage that will allow an employee to maintain a standard of living, usually set by government.

MINOR A person under the age of legal responsibility prescribed by a state.

MIRANDA WARNINGS The constitutional rights afforded a person placed under arrest, such as the right to remain silent, the right to a lawyer, and the right to be informed that any statement made by the prisoner may be used against him. According to the Miranda Rule of 1966, a person placed under arrest must be informed of these rights before questioning.

MISCARRIAGE OF JUSTICE Harm, or injury, inflicted upon an innocent person by a court or public official.

MISCEGENATION Marriage or cohabitation of a man and a woman of different races.

MISCONDUCT OF OFFICE The unlawful or improper behavior of a person while serving as a public officer.

MISDEMEANOR A criminal offense, lesser than a felony, usually punished by a fine or a short jail sentence.

MISFEASANCE The unlawful, improper, or injurious performance of an otherwise lawful act.

MISPRISION 1. In modern times, the failure to report either a felony or valuable information regarding a felony, which could possibly lead to the imprisonment of an innocent suspect for a crime done by another. 2. Misconduct by a public official, especially regarding funds.

MISPRISION OF FELONY The crime of concealing or failing to report a crime.

MISREPRESENTATION Intentional or unintentional false or misleading words or actions.

MISTAKE An error arising out of a misunderstanding.

MISTAKE OF FACT An error that is not the result of negligence.

MISTAKE OF LAW An error in the interpretation of the meaning of a law as it pertains to known facts.

MISTRIAL A trial that is dismissed because of a major mistake or error made during the course of the trial.

MISUSER A person who improperly or unlawfully makes use of a right or misuses an office.

MITIGATING CIRCUMSTANCES Conditions or facts that do not excuse a wrongdoing but reduce the guilt of the defendant or the damages to be awarded the plaintiff.

MITIGATION OF DAMAGES Facts that show that the amount a plaintiff asks the court to award in a lawsuit is excessive and unfair.

Mitter To transfer.

Mittimus 1. A court's order to send a defendant to stand trial in another court. 2. A court's order to send a prisoner to jail.

MODIFICATION Some minor change that improves or otherwise distinguishes itself from an original design.

Modus operandi Method of operation; the manner in which a criminal will commit or attempt to commit a crime.

MOIETY 50 per cent, or half, or something.

MOLESTATION A hostile or harmful interference with someone or something.

MONEY A medium of exchange, such as coins or bills, authorized by the government.

MONOGAMY Marriage with only one person for a lifetime or with only one person at a time.

MONOPOLY Complete (or at least effective) control over the manufacture, price, distribution, and sale of goods or services by one company or by a group of companies acting together.

MORALITY The ethics, conduct, and principles that a society labels as virtuous.

MORAL OBLIGATION The duty or responsibility to act in a just manner, even when not called for by law.

MORAL TURPITUDE Depraved, or vile, conduct; moral corruption that affects society in general.

MORATORIUM A temporary suspension of some activity, ordered by a court.

MORGUE 1. A building to which dead bodies are taken for identification. 2. A newspaper file.

MORTGAGE A conditional conveyance of rights in personal or real property as collateral for a loan.

Mortis causa By reason of death; done by a person who is expecting to die in the near future.

MORTUARY A building where dead bodies are temporarily kept for embalmment.

MOTION A request from one of the parties in a trial that the court act on a certain matter.

MOTION OF CHANGE OF VENUE A request that a case be tried in another locale.

MOTION TO DISMISS A request that a case be thrown out of court.

MOTIVE The cause or reason behind some act.

MOVE To make a motion; to suggest a course of action to a judge.

Multa non vetat lex, quae tamen tacite damnavit "Some things are not forbidden by the law that are nonetheless silently condemned."

Multitudo imperitorum perdit curiam "'A multitude of ignorant lawyers can destroy a court."

MUNICIPAL Pertaining to the government of a city or town.

MUNICIPAL CORPORATION A city-owned company.

MUNIMENTS Written proof of ownership of a piece of land; a deed.

MURDER The willful, unlawful, and unjustified killing of a human being with malice and premeditation.

Mutatis mutandis With the necessary changes in details, especially regarding information that has been brought up to date.

MUTILATION 1. The act of damaging or cutting off parts of another person's body. 2. The damaging of a legal document by removing an essential part from it, by cutting, burning, erasure, etc.

MUTINY An open revolt against authority, especially a revolt among sailors or soldiers against their commanding officers.

MUTUAL Common to two or more parties.

MUTUAL ASSENT An agreement between two or more parties to a contract as to the purpose and terms of the contract.

MUTUAL FUND Stock in a company that buys and sells shares of other companies for profit.

MUTUALITY OF CONTRACT The reciprocal obligations undertaken by the parties to a contract.

MUTUUM A loan whereby the borrower agrees to replace the property he uses with similar items, because by its use the borrowed property will be destroyed.

N

NATURAL LAW A term for laws imposed by nature and reason, rather than by legislation and statutes.

NATURALIZATION The granting of citizenship to an alien.

Ne exeat A court's order preventing a person from leaving the area; a writ forbidding a defendant from leaving a jurisdiction.

NECESSARIES Things needed to maintain human life, although often the financial circumstances of a person are taken into account in deciding just what is necessary.

Nefas Wrong, unjust, against divine law.

NEGLIGENCE The failure to act with reasonable care or to act as a prudent man would to protect the interests of others.

NEGLIGENT HOMICIDE A death resulting from a failure to act with reasonable care while performing a lawful act.

NEGOTIABLE INSTRUMENT A written instrument signed by a person who promises to pay a specified sum of money either on the order of the person whose name appears on the paper or to the person who possesses the paper. The money is payable on demand or at a time specified in writing. Checks, notes, and IOU's are negotiable instruments.

NEGOTIATION 1. The act of reaching an agreement on the terms of a business transaction. 2. The act of putting a negotiable instrument into circulation.

Neminem laedit qui jure suo utitur "He who stands by his rights hurts no one."

Nemo agit in seipsum "No one should bring suit against himself."

Nemo dat qui non habet "No one can give what he doesn't have."

Nemo de domo sua extrahi potest "No one should be dragged from his home."

Nemo debet aliena jactura locupletari "No one should gain from another person's misfortune."

Nemo debet bis puniri pro uno delicto "No one should be punished twice for the same offense."

Nemo debet esse judex in propria causa "No one should be the judge of his own cause."

Nemo est supra leges "No one is above the law."

Nemo praesumitur malus "No one should be presumed to be guilty."

Nemo tenetur ad impossibile "No one can be made to do something that is impossible."

Nemo tenetur seipsum accusare "No one should be made to incriminate himself."

NEPOTISM The practice of giving jobs or patronage to relatives.

NET The portion left after necessary deductions and expenses are taken out.

NET PROFIT What is left after expenses are taken out.

NEXT FRIEND A person, other than a guardian, who brings an action to court for a person who is unable to do so because of age or mental illness.

Nil debet Owing nothing.

Nisi prius The trial court, with judge and jury, in which a case is first heard.

NO FAULT 1. A system allowed in some states whereby an automobile-insurance company will pay a policy owner's claim up to a certain amount, no matter who caused the accident. 2. A divorce in which neither spouse blames the other for causing the breakup of the marriage.

Nolle prosequi A declaration by a prosecutor or a plaintiff that states an unwillingness to continue with the proceedings. Such a declaration does not preclude future action on the matter.

Nolo contendere A plea in which a criminal defendant does not contest the charges being brought against him. This is something less than a plea of guilty, but the defendant may be sentenced on the basis of a *nolo contendere* plea.

NOMINAL In name only, with no physical existence.

NOMINAL DAMAGES A token sum awarded to a party which has not shown itself to have suffered substantial injuries.

NOMINEE 1. Someone who has been suggested or is being considered for the holding of an office. 2. One appointed as a representative for another for a limited, defined purpose.

Non assumpsit A plea in which a defendant argues that an alleged promise the plaintiff seeks to enforce was never made.

Non compos mentis Mentally incompetent.

Non culpabilis (*non cul.*) Not guilty.

Non damnificatus A plea made by a defendant that no injury was done to the plaintiff.

Non decipitur qui scit se decipi "A person who knows that he is being deceived is not really being deceived."

Non est factum A plea that argues that the instrument on which a plaintiff sues was not executed by the defendant.

Non est regula quin fallat "There are exceptions to every law."

Non omne quod licet honestum est "Not everything permitted by the law is honorable."

Non possessori incumbit necessitas probandi possessiones ad se pertinere "A person should not be made to prove that his possessions belong to him."

Non quod dictum est, sed quod factum est inspicitur "Regard not what is said, but what is done."

Non sequitur "It does not follow"; it doesn't make sense; an action or decree that is illogical.

NONACCESS 1. The nonexistence of sexual relations between

spouses. 2. The absence of opportunity for sexual relations between spouses.

NONAGE Under the legal age; the state of infancy.

NONDEADLY FORCE A force that does not normally cause death.

NONDISCLOSURE Failure to divulge facts.

NONFEASANCE Failure to perform certain acts that an agent or official is bound by law or duty to perform.

NONSUIT A judgment for a defendant and against a plaintiff when the plaintiff fails or neglects to prove his case.

NORRIS-LA GUARDIA ACT OF 1932 A federal law prohibiting yellow-dog contracts.

NOT GUILTY A plea in which the defendant states that he did not commit the crime he is being charged with.

Nota A brand burned into a criminal's skin during ancient times, in order to permanently mark him as a lawbreaker.

NOTARY PUBLIC A public officer charged with the duty of certifying the authenticity of documents, and with certain other functions as provided by law.

NOTE A signed document whereby the signer promises to pay a specified amount of money at a specified time.

NOTICE 1. Knowledge of a given fact. 2. Information regarding a fact, sometimes embodied in a document, especially in a trial. 3. A warning.

NOVATION A transfer of a contracted obligation to a third party and consented to by the party to whom the obligation is owed.

Nudum pactum An unenforcible, one-sided promise; a promise made without any consideration.

NUISANCE An annoyance, especially when a person uses his property in a way that interferes with someone else's enjoyment of his own property. Examples: keeping dangerous animals or making loud noises.

NULL Not valid; of no effect.

NULLIFY To make void or render invalid.

Nullius filius Son of no one; a bastard.

NONCUPATIVE WILL An oral or spoken will declared before witnesses, rather than a will made out in writing.

Nuptias non concubitus sed consensus facit "Consent, not cohabitation, makes a marriage."

◀ O ▶

OAS The abbreviation for Organization of American States.

OATH A promise to tell the truth during a judicial proceeding, under the threat of punishment for perjury.

Obiter dictum A statement made in court that does not pertain to the decision of the case.

OBJECTION The act of protesting something on legal grounds.

OBLIGEE A person who is owed some obligation.

OBLIGOR A person who owes an obligation to another.

OBSCENE Damaging to the morality of a community, as defined by various jurisdictions.

OBSCENITY Anything that is found damaging to the morals of a community.

Obstante Obstructing, or blocking.

OBSTRUCTION OF JUSTICE The offense of intentionally preventing, hindering, encumbering, or frustrating the process of justice. For example, anyone who intentionally keeps a witness from testifying at a trial would be obstructing justice.

ODIUM Ill feelings or hatred.

OEO The abbreviation for the Office of Economic Opportunity.

OFFENSE A violation of the criminal law.

OFFENSES AGAINST PROPERTY A term for a group of crimes and civil wrongdoings that result in damage or loss of property belonging to another. Examples would include larceny and arson.

OFFENSES AGAINST THE PERSON A term used to describe a group of crimes and civil wrongdoings that result in physical harm to, or damage to the reputation of, another person. Examples: murder, battery, slander.

OFFENSES AGAINST THE PUBLIC PEACE A term for a group of crimes that result in disturbing the peace and order of a community. Examples: riot, drunkenness.

OFFER A proposition or suggestion to do something that would be a contract if unconditionally accepted by the person to whom it is made.

OFF THE RECORD An unofficial statement.

OFFICER An agent of a public entity.

OMISSION The failure to do something that is required by law or duty.

OMNIBUS A term for two or more independent matters dealt with in a single declaration or legislative bill.

OPEN SEASON A particular time of year set by law when the hunting or fishing of specified species of game or fish is permitted.

OPEN SHOP A business employing both union and nonunion employees.

OPTION The exclusive right to buy something, at a fixed price within a certain time, in exchange for consideration.

ORDER A command issued by a judicial authority; a command by a person with the authority to make commands, such as a police officer.

ORDER OF PERFORMANCE An order by a judge, commanding one of the parties to a lawsuit to do certain things.

ORDINANCE Generally, a law enacted by a city government; however, some federal laws are also known as ordinances.

ORIGINAL JURISDICTION The court in which a case is originally heard.

ORPHAN A child who has lost both parents, because of either death or abandonment.

OSTENSIBLE Visible, or apparent.

OSTENSIBLE PARTNER A person who, by name, appears to be the partner of a business but in truth is not; a figurehead.

OUSTER Wrongful possession of land, which forces the rightful owner to seek remedy at law to regain possession.

OUTLAWED Describing that which has no lawful purpose.

OVERDRAFT The act of overdrawing an account.

OVERDRAW To take more money out of an account than is in the account, especially by writing a check for more than what is in a checking account.

OVERHEAD The costs incurred in relation to the operation of a business.

OVERRULE A judge's rejection of an objection made by one of the parties in a judicial proceeding.

OVERT Uncovered; out in the open.

OYER In modern terms, a copy of an original document that has become the subject of a lawsuit. Such a copy is given to the opposing party.

◀ P ▶

Pacare To make a payment.

Pacatio Payment.

Paci sunt maxime contraria vis et injuria "Violence and injury are the things most hostile to peace."

PACT, OR *pactum* An agreement, or contract; a mutual promise.

PACTIONS Contracts to perform single, specified acts made between two nations.

PACTIONAL Having to do with the formation of an agreement, or pact.

Pactum de non petendo An agreement that one party will not sue the other party.

PADDER A bandit who travels on foot.

PADDY WAGON A van used to transport people who have been arrested to the police station, jail, or court. Paddy is the slang term for an Irishman, and because many Irish immigrants sought employment as police officers, their vehicles became known as "paddy wagons."

PALM OFF To deceitfully impose something on another.

PALMIST A fortuneteller who claims to tell a person's future by reading the person's palm.

PALPABLE Obvious, noticeable, readily observed.

PANDER To procure women for the purpose of prostitution.

PANDERER A person who procures women for the purpose of prostitution.

PANEL A list of people, summoned by a sheriff, from which a jury will be chosen.

PAPER A document; a legal instrument.

PAR 1. The face value of securities or the price at which

they are issued. 2. The established value of the monetary unit of one country expressed in terms of the monetary unit of another country.

Par delictum Equal guilt; both parties in a lawsuit have been found equally at fault and the court will favor neither.

Par in parem imperium non habet "An equal has no right to control an equal."

PARAPH 1. A signature. 2. A design or flourish added to a signature in an effort to prevent someone else from trying to forge the signature.

PARCENARY Pertaining to the holding of an estate of real property by two or more heirs before the inheritance is divided.

PARCENER An heir who shares an estate of land with other heirs.

PARCHMENT A durable paper made of lambskin, historically used for legal documents.

PARDON The deliverance of a convict from punishment dealt by the courts and restoration of his civil rights, by order of a high public officer empowered with the right to grant pardons. A pardoned offender stands in the eyes of the law as if he had never committed the offense.

Parens patriae A nation's right to supervise its children and others who are legally unable to supervise themselves.

PARENT A mother or father.

PARENTICIDE The crime of killing one's own parent.

Parentum est liberos alere etiam nothos "It is the parents' duty to support their children even if they are illegitimate."

Pari delicto Equal in guilt, or fault.

Pari materia On the same subject.

Pari passu Equal and without preference.

PARISH A civil division, in the state of Louisiana, corresponding to a county in other states.

PAROLE The release of a prisoner from prison for good behavior before the completion of his sentence, on his word that he will continue to act lawfully.

PAROL EVIDENCE Oral statements made when two or more parties enter a written contract. Parol evidence is not admitted as evidence if it is inconsistent with the written contract.

PARQUET In France, the judges who hear criminal cases.

Pars gravata The aggrieved party; the injured party in a lawsuit.

Particeps criminis A partner in crime.

PARTICULARS The details of a lawsuit.

PARTNERSHIP A contractual relationship between two or more persons who take part in a business venture and share in its profits and losses.

PART PERFORMANCE The performance of part of one's contractual duties.

Partus sequitur ventrem "The offspring of an animal belongs to the owner of the mother."

PARTY A person or organization that takes part or has an interest in any matter, affair, or proceeding.

PARTY WALL A wall built between two pieces of property and owned in common by the neighboring landowners.

Parum est lantam esse sententiam nisi mandetur executioni "There is little reason to pass judgment if it will not be enforced."

PASS 1. To pronounce judgment. 2. To have been successfully examined. 3. To distribute or spread around. 4. To travel.

PASSAGE 1. The traveling over water or land. 2. The enacting of a bill into law by the legislature.

PASSBOOK A book in which a bank customer's deposits and withdrawals are recorded.

PASSION An emotion that renders the mind incapable of rational thought and deliberation. "Crimes of passion" are crimes committed by a person temporarily rendered incapable of rational thought.

PAST CONSIDERATION That which is given or done before a contract is made. Past consideration cannot later be used to satisfy the consideration given in exchange for a promise in a contract.

PATENT 1. (n.) An exclusive grant or privilege made by a government to a person or persons; usually refers to land grants or to the exclusive rights to an invention given an inventor for a period of time. 2. (adj.) That which is obvious.

PATENT DEFECTS Defects in merchandise that are clearly visible.

PATENT RIGHTS Those rights obtained by a patent holder, usually the exclusive right to make and sell a patented item.

PATENTEE A person who has been granted a patent.

PATERNAL POWER The lawful authority parents have over their children.

PATERNITY SUIT A lawsuit charging a man with being the father of a woman's child and requesting child support.

Pari ratione For the same reason.

PATIBULARY Pertaining to the gallows.

PATIBULUM The Old English word for gallows.

PATRICIDE The killing of one's own father.

PAUPER A destitute person; a person with little or no money.

PAWN To put something up as security for a borrowed sum.

PAWNBROKER A person whose business is lending money on items of personal property, which he keeps in his shop until the loan is paid and the item redeemed.

PAYEE A person who receives a note or check made payable to him in money or goods.

PAYOR, OR PAYER A person who makes a note or check for the purpose of paying another.

PEACE The absence of war, violence, or disturbance of public order; quiet, serenity.

Peccata contra naturam sunt gravissima "Crimes against nature are the most serious."

PECULATION The unlawful spending of public money entrusted to one's care.

Peculatus The crime of embezzling public money.

PECUNIARY 1. Consisting of what can be valued in money. 2. Having to do with money.

PECUNIARY LOSS A loss of money.

PEDESTRIAN A person who is walking.

Pedis abscisso An old method of punishment consisting of cutting off a prisoner's foot.

PEEPING TOM A person in the habit of peering into other peoples' windows in a sneaky manner, usually for the purpose of invading the occupant's privacy.

PENAL Having to do with penalties.

PENAL CODE A collection of laws that, if violated, provide for a penalty to be dealt out by the courts. Penal codes deal with offenses of a public nature.

PENALTY 1. A punishment inflicted for some violation of the law. 2. Money paid to another because of some breach of contract.

Pendente lite Pending a decision by a court; during litigation.

Pendentes Latin for crops in the field "pending" harvest.

PENDING Not yet decided.

PENITENTIARY A prison where criminals are sent by the courts.

PENSION An allowance given by a government for services rendered by an individual.

PENSIONER A person who lives on a pension.

Per annum Yearly; by the year; once a year.

Per capita By the head; a term used in wills to indicate that an estate is to be divided among the decedent's issue equally, regardless of degree of kinship. (I.e., an inheriting child and an inheriting grandchild would receive equal shares.) The opposite of *per stirpes*.

Per curiam By the court; an entire court's opinion of a case, as opposed to a majority opinion or a minority opinion.

Per diem Once a day; by the day; daily.

Per se By itself.

PER CENT One of one hundred; for example, 1 per cent of one dollar is one cent.

PEREMPTORY Absolute; mandatory.

PERFORM To complete or fulfill (some obligation).

PERFORMANCE The completion or fulfillment (of some obligation, undertaking or contract).

PERJURY The crime of willfully making a false statement under oath.

PERISHABLE COMMODITY OR GOOD A product that loses value if not quickly used, such as milk, fresh fruit, and eggs.

PERMANENT DISABILITY A term, usually found in insurance policies, describing a disability or handicap that the policyholder would suffer with for the rest of his life.

PERMISSION The authority to do something that would be unlawful without such authority.

PERMISSIVE Readily giving permission or consent.

PERMIT An oral or written authorization to perform an act that would otherwise be unlawful.

PERNANCY Taking or receiving something of value.

PERPETRATE To perform or commit (some act).

PERPETRATOR A person who leads others in the commission of a crime; one who actually commits a crime.

PERPETUITY Eternity. The term specifically refers to a decedent's attempt to control the use of his estate beyond the lifespan of his heir.

Persona non grata The status of a diplomat who is not personally acceptable to the government of the country he has been sent to.

PERSONAL EFFECTS Personal property, especially items carried on the person.

PERSONAL INJURY An injury to the body.

PERSONAL PROPERTY, OR PERSONALTY Anything movable that can be owned, other than real property.

Per stirpes Opposite of *per capita.* A term used in wills to indicate that inheriting grandchildren receive a share of an estate equal to that which their parent would have received were he or she alive.

PERTAINING Having to do with; belonging to; relating to.

PERTINENT Important; relevant.

Pessimi exempli A horrible example.

PETIT JURY A jury selected for the trial of a civil or criminal action.

PETITION A request in writing, made to a court or a public officer, to do something, especially to redress a wrong.

PETTY Of lesser importance.

PETTY LARCENY The unlawful taking and carrying away of the property of another that has less value than the amount determined by law to constitute grand larceny.

PETTY OFFENSE Generally, a minor infraction of some ordinance.

PHYSICAL FACT Evidence that can be seen, heard, or felt. Example: a gunshot.

PHYSICAL IMPOSSIBILITY Something that cannot possibly be done.

PICKPOCKET A thief who steals from the pockets of unknowing victims.

PILFER To steal, specifically in small amounts so that the loss will go unnoticed.

PILFERAGE 1. Losses that result from the theft of small amounts of goods, especially merchandise being transported. 2. The practice of stealing in small amounts so the thefts will go unnoticed.

PILFERER One who pilfers.

PILLAGE The forcible taking of private property by an invading army.

PIMP A panderer.

PIRACY Banditlike conduct on the high seas.

Pirata est hostis humani generis "A pirate is hostile to all mankind."

PIRATE A person guilty of piracy; a robber of ships at sea.

PIT AND GALLOWS The privilege granted by the King of Scotland to the victim of a theft enabling the victim personally to execute the thief. In such cases, women were drowned in a pit, while men were hanged from the gallows.

PITTANCE A bite to eat or a small allowance, handed out at festivals.

PLACE OF CONTRACT The state where a contract agreement is entered into. The contract is subject to the laws of that state.

PLAGIARISM The publication of another person's work—in whole or in part—and claiming it as one's own.

PLAINTIFF A person who brings a lawsuit or complaint to court; a person who brings a court action against a defendant.

PLAINTIFF IN ERROR A person who sues to have some judgment or legal process reviewed.

PLAT A map of a piece of land, with streets and lots shown.

PLEA 1. A defendant's answer to the charges brought against him in a criminal court. 2. The formal, written statement of the facts and claims of a case to be answered by the other party in a civil case.

PLEAD 1. To file a plea. 2. To argue a case before a judge.

PLEADING A legal process whereby one party in court makes a written claim to be answered by the other party, who in turn states his claim to be answered by the one. This defines and narrows the issues in controversy.

PLEDGE 1. Something delivered to another to hold as security for the payment of a debt or obligation. 2. A promise.

PLEDGEE The party to whom something is pledged.

PLEDGOR A party who makes a pledge.

PLUNDER The capture of personal property belonging to an enemy.

POACHING The stealing or unlawful hunting of poultry or game animals.

POISON A substance that, when taken into the body, is capable of causing death.

POLICE POWER The power of a state government to enforce laws protecting the health, safety, and welfare of its people.

POLICY 1. The purpose or tendency of some law or rule, usually in reference to the well-being of society. 2. A course of action. 3. A contract of insurance.

POLTROON A coward.

POLYANDRY The practice of having two or more husbands at the same time.

POLYGAMY The practice of having two or more spouses at the same time.

POLYGYNY The practice of having two or more wives at the same time.

POOR LAWS English laws concerned with providing relief for paupers.

PORT OF ENTRY A border post, seaport, or airport where travelers and goods can legally enter a country from abroad.

Portio legitima A part of an inheritance that is due one's children and that cannot be denied, even by the will of the decedent.

POSITIVE EVIDENCE Information that has been proved to be true and that has established the truth or falsehood of the point at issue.

Posse 1. That which is possible. 2. Popular abbreviation of *posse comitatus*.

Posse comitatus Citizens organized under the direction of a sheriff to help in keeping the peace or to assist in capturing felons.

POSSESS To have under physical control.

POSSESSION That which is under a person's physical control.

POSSESSORY Having to do with the right to possess.

POSSESSORY ACTION A court hearing held to determine which party has the right to possess a piece of real property.

POSTDATE To date (an instrument) with a date later than when the instrument is actually made.

Post-mortem EXAMINATION The examination of a corpse in order to find the cause of death; an autopsy.

Potentia non est nisi ad bonum "Power is conferred for no other reason than the good of the public."

POWER OF APPOINTMENT An authority given by deed or will enabling the holder to select who will enjoy a given piece of property.

POWER OF ATTORNEY A written statement authorizing an agent to act on behalf of the person whose signature appears on the document.

PRAYER, OR COMPLAINT A request made by a plaintiff that the court grant him relief from the wrong being complained of.

PRECATORY WORDS Words requesting something, rather than ordering it.

PRECEDENT A case or opinion that is used as an example for reaching a similar result when similar facts arise.

PRECINCT A neighborhood or area, with distinct boundaries, which is established for the efficient administration of a public service, especially police, firefighting, or voting.

PREFERRED STOCK Stock in a corporation whose holders are usually paid dividends before the holders of other (common) stock.

PREJUDICE Partiality; preconceived opinions for or against something.

PREJUDICED WITNESS A witness with preconceived opinions on the facts of a case and who gives biased testimony in court.

PRELIMINARY EXAMINATION A hearing for the purpose of examining the evidence against the party charged.

PRELIMINARY INJUNCTION An immediate injunction to stop the defendant from doing that which the plaintiff has complained of until the case has been heard and the judgment rendered.

PRELIMINARY NEGOTIATIONS Communication between two parties before a contractual relationship is begun.

PREMEDITATION The intent formed in advance to commit an act.

PREMISE The proposition from which a conclusion is deduced.

PREMISES Real property.

PREMIUM A reward, bounty, or bonus for some act.

PREPAYMENT Payment before it becomes due.

PREPONDERANCE OF EVIDENCE Evidence that has the greater weight or that is the more convincing.

PRESCRIPTION The gaining of rights or title to a piece of real property by virture of uninterrupted use of the property over a period of time set by state law.

PRESUMPTION A conclusion or inference drawn from an examination of facts surrounding an issue that do not in themselves provide an answer.

PRETERMIT To disregard or fail to mention one's children in a will.

PREVENTION The act of hindering or stopping.

PRICE That which is paid for the use, pleasure, or ownership of something.

PRICE DISCRIMINATION The practice of charging various prices to various customers for the same goods, or selling to one customer and not to another.

Prima facie On the face; that which is taken as true until disproved by evidence.

PRIMARY EVIDENCE The evidence that gives the greatest certainty. Example: A document is the primary evidence of its content.

PRINCIPAL 1. (adj.) Most important or original. 2. (n.) A person who is bound by an obligation. 3. The perpetrator of a crime. 4. The sum of money, other than interest, which is needed to pay off debt. 5. The employer of an agent.

PRINCIPLE OF LAW A rule, doctrine, or abstract generalization regarding the law.

PRIORITIES Those things that have a prior right and must be dealt with before others.

PRIORITY A right that comes before others.

PRIVACY The state of being let alone or free of unwanted publicity.

PRIVATE PERSON A person not in public office.

PRIVILEGE 1. An advantage. 2. A right to do something. 3. An exemption from some duty.

PRIVILEGE AGAINST SELF-INCRIMINATION A constitutional right of a person to refuse to give testimony that might incriminate him.

PRIVILEGED COMMUNICATION Statements that cannot be made the basis for recovery of damages in a libel or slander suit because of the relationship of the parties involved to each other or to the subject matter of the statements. Examples: statements made during the course of a lawsuit by the judge, counsel, witnesses, or parties to the action; statements made by members of a legislative body in the course of their duty. A fair report by a newspaper of a judicial or legislative proceeding is also privileged, but if hostility or real malice is shown, such a statement is not privileged.

PRIVITY 1. Inside knowledge. 2. Mutual or successive interests in property.

PRIVITY OF CONTRACT The relationship between the parties to a contract, giving rise to rights and duties.

PROBABLE CAUSE Reasonable cause; a reasonable ground for believing the facts alleged.

PROBATE Proof, submitted to a judge, that a will left by a decedent is genuine.

Pro bono publico For the public good.

PROBATION Relief of a convict from all or part of his prison term on the condition that he behave lawfully and remain under supervision.

PROCEDURE The method and manner in which a case is brought to court and tried.

PROCESS 1. The manner in which a court enforces compliance with its orders. 2. In patent law, any method used to obtain certain rights.

PROCESS SERVER A person employed to deliver to another a writ or summons ordering an appearance in court.

PROCURATION The act of authorizing another to act as one's agent.

PRODUCT LIABILITY An area within the law of torts concerned with the liability of a manufacturer who places a defective product on the market.

PROFESSIONAL LIABILITY That duty, obligation, or responsibility to which a professional person is held answerable.

PROFESSIONAL NEGLIGENCE Negligence resulting from a breach of the higher standard of care required of professionals.

PROFITEERING The pursuit of excessive profits at the expense of one's reputation or professional responsibility.

PROMISE A statement that obligates the maker of the statement, either legally, as in a contract, or morally—if there is consideration involved.

PROMISSORY ESTOPPEL A legal principle whereby if one party is induced to rely on the promise of another to his detriment, the promising party can be held liable.

PROMISSORY NOTE A written promise to pay a specified sum of money, either on demand of the person holding the note or after a specified date.

PROMOTER A person who forms a corporation.

PROOF Anything that a jury chooses to accept as evidence establishing the truth of an allegation.

PROOF OF CLAIM A sworn statement made by an insurance claimant describing the time and manner of the loss he is claiming.

PROPERTY That which can be owned; the right to exclusive possession or enjoyment of a thing.

PROPOSAL An offer, request, suggestion, or plan.

PROPOSITION The statement of a proposal or scheme.

PROSECUTION The act of bringing suit against a person charged with the commission of some civil or criminal wrongdoing or liability.

PROSECUTOR A person entrusted with bringing court action against those suspected of being guilty of crimes against the people.

PROSPECTIVE Looking toward, or effective in, the future.

PROSPECTUS A document published for the purpose of interesting prospective investors in investing in a business or venture.

PROSTITUTE A woman who engages in sexual intercourse for money.

PROSTITUTION The crime, in most states, of offering to perform sexual acts with another for money.

Pro tanto For so much; to such an extent.

PROTEST 1. A written statement calling into question the lawfulness or fairness of some act or statement. 2. Notice that a negotiable instrument was refused payment.

PROVISIONAL Temporary; providing for a temporary need but subject to change.

PROVOCATION The act of tempting, enticing, or stimulating another to perform a particular deed or act, usually an illegal one.

PROXIMATE CAUSE Something that produces a result in the natural sequence of events; the necessary factor causing a result that stands closest to that result.

PROXY A person who represents another, who is absent; an instrument containing the appointment of such a person.

PRUDENCE Wisdom; care; watchfulness.

PUBLICATION 1. The offering of anything to the public at large. In defamation cases, communication to one person qualifies as publication. 2. A printed book, circular, magazine, or newspaper.

PUBLICATION OF SUMMONS The advertising of a summons in a newspaper to notify a defendant that court proceedings are being started against him, in cases where the defendant cannot be notified in person.

PUBLIC AUTHORITY That which is created and empowered to act on behalf of the citizens of a state, county, city, or nation. Examples include municipal transportation authorities, the Tennessee Valley Authority, etc.

PUBLIC ENTITY An agency or department created by the authority of a federal, state, county, or municipal government.

PUBLIC POLICY A principal of law whereby no person can lawfully behave in a way that endangers the general public.

PUBLIC TORT A wrongdoing against the public.

PUBLIC TRIAL A court trial that any member of the public may attend.

PUBLIC-WELFARE OFFENSE A violation of the regulations that exist for the public welfare.

PUBLISH To make public. To make available to the public, either by printing and distributing or by speaking in public. In libel or defamation cases, communication to one person qualifies as publishing.

PUNITIVE Having to do with punishment.

PUNITIVE DAMAGES Money awarded to a plaintiff by a court for the purpose of inflicting punishment on the defendant.

PURCHASE-MONEY MORTGAGE A loan by a seller enabling someone to buy the seller's property, which then becomes security for the loan.

PURLOIN To steal or pilfer.

PURPORT Meaning, purpose, or objective.

PUTATIVE MARRIAGE A marriage performed in ignorance of the existence of something that renders it unlawful.

◀ Q ▶

Qua As; in the character of; in the capacity of.

QUALIFY 1. To prepare. 2. To restrict or limit.

Quantum damnificatus Literally, How much damnified? A question asked of the plaintiff by the court, in order to determine the amount of compensation.

Quantum meruit The value of one's work; an action for recovery based not on a contract but on an implied promise to pay for the reasonable worth of work done up to a certain point.

QUARANTINE The lawful detention or isolation of people and animals that have been exposed to contagious diseases, in order to prevent the disease from spreading.

QUASH To annul or make void; invalidate.

Quasi As if; similar.

QUASI CONTRACT A contractual obligation springing from a mutual relationship between the parties, rather than from an expressed contract. An implied, rather than a stated contract.

Quasi-in-rem Proceedings brought against a defendant although the real object of the action is a particular piece of property; also used for getting jurisdiction in certain instances when a person can't be dealt with but his property can be.

QUEEN'S BENCH The highest court in England. When a king is the ruling monarch, it is called King's Bench.

Qui destruit medium destruit finem "He who destroys the means, destroys the end."

Qui in utero est pro jam nato habetur, quoties de ejus comodo quaeritur "A child in the womb should be considered already born, whenever his benefit is at issue."

Qui male agit odit lucem "He who acts wrongly hates the light"; a lawbreaker prefers to act in secret.

Qui mandat ipse fecissi videtur "A party who commands a thing to be done is seen as having done it himself."

Qui parcit nocentibus innocentes punit "He who spares the guilty punishes the innocent."

Quid pro quo Something given for something; mutual consideration in a contract.

QUIET ENJOYMENT A right given to a tenant in a lease allowing him to receive and enjoy peaceably what he has rented.

QUITCLAIM The name given an agreement by which one party gives whatever rights he had in property to another.

Quod dubitas, ne feceris "When in doubt about something, don't do it."

Quod hoc As to this.

Quod necessitas cogit, excusat "A person who is forced to commit a crime will be excused."

Quod ultra As to the rest.

Quod vanum et inutile est, lex non requirit "What is vain and useless will not be required by the law."

QUORUM The minimum number of people attending a meeting in order for the meeting to validly transact business.

QUOTATION 1. The stated price of an item. 2. An exact, word-for-word printed duplication or oral repetition of a statement from some authority.

◂ R ▸

RAPE The crime of having unlawful sexual intercourse with a woman without her consent.

RATIFICATION The act of confirming, supporting, or approving of an act done earlier or by another.

Ratio decidendi The ground of a court's decision.

Ratio legis est anima legis "The reason for law is the life of law"; if there were no reason for laws, there would be no laws.

RATIONAL DOUBT (REASONABLE DOUBT) A doubt drawn by an ordinary, reasonable man.

RATTENING The theft of a workman's tools or clothes to harass and coerce the workman into joining a labor union.

RAVISH To rape.

REAL ESTATE AND REAL PROPERTY Land and everything growing or erected on it, including things permanently attached to it.

REAL EVIDENCE Evidence furnished by things themselves. Example: the physical appearance of a person.

REALTY Real estate; land and buildings.

REBATE A discount or reduction in the price of something, usually given back to the payer after the full price has been paid.

REBUT To bar, disprove, or repel, especially a claim or accusation.

REBUTTABLE (Something) that can be disputed or argued; (something) that is presumed but not proved.

RECALL A procedure for removing an elected official from office before the end of his term through a vote of the electorate.

RECEIPT A written statement showing that something has been paid for.

RECEIVER A person appointed by a court to take care of money or property under legal dispute or when the holder of title is incompetent.

RECEIVER *pendente lite* A responsible, impartial person named by the court to receive income from property while a case is undecided.

RECEIVERSHIP An act by a court, placing disputed property or money in the care of a third party (receiver) until the dispute is settled. Often used when a business has suffered a great loss.

RECEIVING STOLEN PROPERTY The crime of knowingly buying or hiding stolen, embezzled, or extorted goods.

RECIDIVIST A habitual criminal.

RECKLESS Careless, foolhardy—especially where danger to life or safety is an issue.

RECKLESS DRIVING The offense of driving an automobile without regard to others' safety.

RECOGNIZANCE A defendant's obligation, recorded by a court; usually, to appear for trial.

RECONCILIATION The mending of a broken relationship between two people, usually implying forgiveness for past injuries.

RECONVEYANCE The transfer of title, to a piece of land or real property, back to a previous owner. Example: After a mortgage is paid off, the mortgage company transfers the title back to the person who took out the mortgage.

RECORD A formal written account or history of some act, preserved and made available to the public.

RECORDING The filing of deeds, liens, mortgages, etc., in a public place, to give notice to interested parties.

RECOUP 1. To recover. 2. To receive compensation for one's losses.

RECOUPMENT A defendant's right to make a counterclaim against a plaintiff in a civil suit, which will reduce the amount of the plaintiff's claim.

RECOVER 1. To regain or acquire something that had been lost. 2. To obtain compensation for damages or injuries through the legal system. 3. To return to a normal condition.

RECOVERY That which is awarded by courts to a defendant.

RECRIMINATION A countercharge made by a defendant against a plaintiff, particularly in a divorce case.

REDEMPTION The buying back, or repurchasing, of something.

REDRESS Satisfaction or payment awarded by a court for injury or damages suffered by the plaintiff.

REFEREE An official, usually a judge, appointed to hear arguments and claims and to serve as an arbitrator. A judge in a juvenile court is also called a referee.

REFEREE IN BANKRUPTCY A court-appointed officer who deals with administrative matters in a bankruptcy proceeding.

REFERENDUM The placing of a proposed law on a ballot, giving the people, rather than a legislature, a chance to decide.

REFORMATION The rewriting of a contract by a court when the original contract is said to be misleading or does not express the real agreement of the parties.

Regina The Queen of England; *Regina* v. *Riley* really means *The Queen* v. *Riley.*

REGISTRATION OF STOCK Recording in the corporation's official book the name and address of each holder of stock.

REGISTRY The office where books recording details such as ships' names, automobile ownership, animal bloodlines, and other information are kept.

REHABILITATION The restoration of a former ability. Example: To rehabilitate a stroke victim might include teaching the victim to walk again; a criminal would be taught a lawful trade.

REHEARING The second hearing of an argument that has been already decided, in order to present new evidence or to correct an error made in the course of the first hearing.

REIMBURSE To pay back money belonging to another; to repay.

RELATOR A person who provides the state with information necessary to begin court proceedings against someone.

RELEASE The giving up or discharge of a right, claim, or privilege.

RELEASE ON ONE'S OWN RECOGNIZANCE A release obtained from a judge by a prisoner who, in place of bail, swears to abide by the law.

RELEVANT To the point; describing that which deals with the matter in question in a case.

RELIANCE Dependence or trust upon the word or acts (of another).

RELIEF The help, or assistance, given by the court to a wronged or injured party.

RELINQUISHMENT The abandonment, or giving up, of some right or thing.

REMAINDER 1. That which is left. 2. That part of an estate left after claims and provisions of a will, or prior interest in property, have been met.

REMEDIAL STATUTE 1. A new law, passed to correct a mistake in a previous law. 2. A law providing a remedy that did not exist before.

REMEDY A legal cure for some wrongdoing.

REMITTANCE A cash, check, or money order sent to another person.

Remittitur 1. The appellate court's denial of a new trial for a defendant when a plaintiff agrees to accept less money than what was awarded. 2. A judge's order decreasing the money awarded by a jury to a plaintiff. 3. An appellate court's sending back of a case to the original court for a new trial.

Remittitur damnum "The damage is remitted." A declaration, entered on the court record, whereby a plaintiff agrees to give up damages awarded him by a jury in excess of the amount originally sought.

RENT Payment made to the owner of property by a tenant for the use of that property.

RENTER A person who pays rent for something.

RENT STRIKE The refusal to pay rent, as a form of protest by renters, usually for a diminishment in services.

Renvoi (Fr.) 1. The escorting of foreign or out-of-state criminals to their own country or state. 2. The practice of drawing upon foreign laws and cases in order to decide a court dispute.

REPARABLE INJURY An injury or wrongdoing that can be compensated by payment of money.

REPEAT OFFENDER A person who repeatedly commits crimes.

REPLEVIN A lawsuit to recover property (rather than compensation) that was unlawfully taken from, or denied to, a plaintiff who owns or has an interest in the property being withheld.

REPORTER 1. A person who makes a record of everything said during a trial; a court reporter. 2. A series of books that report court decisions within a state, territory, or jurisdiction.

REPOSSESS To take back something that has not been paid for. Example: A finance company takes possession of (or repossesses) an automobile if the payments are late.

REPRIEVE The suspension of a death sentence.

REPUBLICATION The re-establishment by a testator of a will he previously revoked.

REPUDIATION A refusal to do something; the renunciation of a right.

REPUGNANT Contrary; incompatible.

REQUIRE To order; to demand.

REQUIREMENTS CONTRACT A contract in which the exact

amount of the goods needed by a contracting party is not specified at the time the contract is made; instead, the contract states that the goods will be delivered as required.

Res communes Things of the community; those things that cannot be possessed exclusively for one person's use.

Res gestae Things that are done during the course of a transaction.

Res integra A matter that has not yet been decided.

Res ipsa loquitur, OR R.I.L. It speaks for itself. A term used for a situation in which a defendant's negligence can be assumed by the court, thereby placing the burden of proof on the defendant to show he was not negligent.

Res judicata A final and conclusive judgment of a case.

Res nullius naturalite fit primi occupantis "That which has no owner naturally belongs to the first to find it."

RESCIND To cancel, annul, or make void.

RESCISSION The canceling of a contract for reasons that are acceptable to the parties to the contract, or as determined by a court, or because of fraud.

RESCUE DOCTRINE A rule that anyone who attempts to rescue another can recover from the negligent person who put the victim in danger, should the rescuer be harmed in the course of the rescue.

RESIDENCE The place where one lives, although perhaps temporarily.

RESIDUARY Left over.

RESIDUARY DEVISEE Someone to whom the remainder of an estate of real property is left, after the other instructions of the will are complied with.

RESIDUARY LEGATEE Someone to whom the remaining personal property in an estate is left, after the other instructions of the will are complied with.

Residuum Literally, residue. That which is left behind.

Respondeat superior A rule charging an employer with the responsibility for the acts of his employees in the scope of their work; literally, let the master answer.

RESPONDENT A person against whom action is taken in an appellate court.

RESPONSIBILITY Legal liability for some act or thing.

RESTITUTION A legal remedy that places both parties in the condition they were in before entering a contract that cannot be completed.

RESTRAINING ORDER A court order to prevent a person from doing something until a hearing can be arranged.

RESTRICT To limit or confine.

RESTRICTIVE COVENANT A clause in a deed that limits the use of the property by the new owner and by the late owners.

RESTRICTIVE ENDORSEMENT An endorsement of a negotiable instrument that limits the negotiable value of the instrument. Example: "for deposit only" on a check.

RETAINER A fee paid by a client when hiring a lawyer, supposedly to prevent that lawyer from working for an adversary.

RETRACT 1. To withdraw, revoke, or cancel. 2. To acknowledge the falseness or error of one's own statements or opinions.

RETROSPECTIVE A term used for a law that affects previous actions done before the law took effect.

REVERSE A higher court's ruling that is contrary to a decision of a lower court and that supplants that decision.

REVERSE DISCRIMINATION Discriminating against one group of people to make amends for discrimination against another group in the past.

REVERT 1. To return to a former state or condition. 2. With respect to property, to return to a former owner or his heirs.

REVOCATION A lawful cancellation of an offer, a legal privilege, or a document.

REWARD A prize that is offered in return for some meritorious act.

REX The King of England; *Rex* v. *Walsh* really means *The King* v. *Walsh.*

Rex non potest peccare "The king can do no wrong."

RIDER A clause that has been added to a legislative bill, contract, or insurance policy.

RIGHT 1. That which is morally and ethically proper. 2. A privilege that is guaranteed by law.

RIGHT OF ACTION The legal right to maintain an action to enforce a claim.

RIGHT OF WAY The right to pass over the land of another, which arises out of either a contractual relationship or an act of law.

RIGHT TO COUNSEL The right of a person to have an attorney represent him in court.

RIGHT-TO-WORK LAWS State laws that prohibit unions from forcing workers to join a union in order to work.

RIOT A disturbance of the peace by three or more people employing or threatening force or violence.

RIPARIAN RIGHTS Privileges that go with a piece of land that borders, or has running through it, a river, stream, or other body of water. (See LITTORAL RIGHTS)

RISK A danger, or hazard.

ROBBERY The illegal taking of another's property by force or violence.

ROLL A list of people's names.

ROOMER A person who rents a room.

ROYALTY Payments made for the use of something, especially a patent or copyrighted material such as a book or a piece of music.

RULE 1. An established standard. 2. An order by a court of law or some other lawfully empowered authority.

RULE AGAINST PERPETUITIES A principle that prevents controls being placed on the ownership of real property for too long a period.

S

SAID Previously mentioned; named earlier.

SALE The transfer of title and possession from a seller to a buyer in exchange for money.

SALES CREDIT Credit that is provided by a seller who honors credit cards.

SALVAGE 1. (v.) To recover (something). 2. (n.) Property that has been recovered from an accident or disaster that has been previously used.

SANCTION 1. (v.) To approve or assent to the acts of another. 2. (n.) A penalty used to make people obey the law.

SANCTUARY 1. A safe place. 2. A place where certain privileges or immunities are available that cannot be had elsewhere.

SATISFACTION The settlement of some obligation, either through payment or through some other act.

SAVING 1. Safekeeping. 2. Preservation from harm or loss.

SAVINGS AND LOAN ASSOCIATION A financial organization in which money deposited by customers is invested in real estate loans.

SCAB A laborer who takes the job of a union member who is out on strike against an employer.

SCHEDULE A calender, or list, especially a list of cases to be heard by a judge.

Scienter Knowledge; a term often used to refer to a defendant's knowledge that his acts would result in injury.

Scilicet (abbreviated as SC) Let it be known. Often used in affidavits and other legal documents.

SCINTILLA The least amount (of evidence needed to support a verdict from a jury).

Scire facias "Cause to know." A judge's order that a defendant show why some record or document should not be allowed to be used in court by the plaintiff.

SCOPE OF EMPLOYMENT What a person has been hired to do or what he does with his employer's consent.

SCROLL A mark or initial made with a pen used in place of a seal.

SEAL An impression that is affixed to a document for the purpose of showing that the document is authentic.

SEARCH The examination or exploration of a person, his home, or his property for the purpose of finding evidence, stolen property, or contraband.

SEARCH AND SEIZURE An area of the law dealing with the police practice of searching a person for evidence, seizing evidence, and the limitations imposed on searches by police by the Fourth and Fourteenth amendments of the Constitution.

SEARCH WARRANT Written permission granted by a judge or magistrate authorizing police officers to search a place for the purpose of finding evidence, stolen property, or contraband.

SECONDARY BOYCOTT A boycott against a company that does business with a company being boycotted.

SECONDARY EVIDENCE Evidence that doesn't come from a primary source. Example: a copy of a contract, used to show what is in the contract.

SECRETARY OF STATE 1. The head of the Department of State of the United States. 2. An official of a state government usually responsible for licensing corporations in his state.

Secundum According to.

Secundum aequum et bonum According to what is just and right.

Secundum bonos mores According to good morals, or established custom.

Secundum formam statuti According to the form of statutory law.

Secundum legem communem According to common law.

SECURED CREDITOR A creditor who holds something that belongs to a debtor, thus assuring that the debt will be paid.

SECURITIES Stocks, bonds, or notes showing ownership in a company; any evidence of debt or property ownership.

SECURITIES AND EXCHANGE COMMISSION (SEC) A federal agency regulating the issuance and sale of stocks and bonds.

SECURITY 1. Something belonging to a debtor that is held by a creditor until the debt is paid. Example: a deposit or a lien. 2. A bond or a certificate of stock. 3. Safety.

SEDITION The crime of stirring up armed resistance against the government; a person can be charged with sedition without having committed an overt act in that direction.

SEDUCTION The act of enticing or luring someone into unlawful sexual relations.

SEISIN Full ownership and possession of a piece of property.

SEIZURE The taking of property, usually by a government official.

SELF-DEFENSE The right to protect one's person, family, or property from harm or destruction at the hands of an assailant. The amount of force that may be used to repel the assailant depends on the particular situation.

SELF-INCRIMINATION, THE RIGHT AGAINST A constitutional right, guaranteed by the Fifth Amendment, whereby a person may refuse to answer any questions asked by authorities if the answers to such questions would tend to involve that person in the crime being charged.

SELLER A person who sells something.

SENTENCE A postconviction judgment, against the defendant in a criminal trial, that sets out the punishment to be inflicted.

SEPARATE MAINTENANCE Money paid by a married person

for the support of a spouse (and children, if any), even though the couple are no longer living together.

SEPARATE PROPERTY Property owned by a married person in his or her own right.

SEPARATED The condition of a married couple who have agreed not to live together.

SEPARATION AGREEMENT A document, often made up when a couple separate, outlining which spouse gets which items of the household and which spouse is to pay the bills.

SEPARATION OF POWERS A term for the division of the U. S. Government into three branches—the legislative, the judicial, and the executive—which, with its built-in system of checks and balances, effectively limits the power of government.

SEQUESTER 1. To isolate a jury. 2. To place property that is under dispute into the hands of a third party to hold until the question of ownership is settled.

Sequi debet potentia justitiam non praecedere "Power should follow justice, not precede it."

Seriatim Separately, individually.

SERVICE OF PROCESS The delivery to a defendant of an official notice requiring him to appear in court.

SERVICE OF SUMMONS BY PUBLICATION The notification of a defendant to appear in court by publishing the notice in a newspaper—permitted when the defendant cannot be served personally with the notice.

SERVIENT Pertaining to land that is somehow restricted in its use by the owners of adjoining property.

SERVITUDE 1. Slavery. 2. A restriction placed on real property belonging to one person for the benefit of others, usually adjoining property owners.

SESSION A period of time, especially a period of time in which court cases are being heard.

SET ASIDE To overrule (a lower court's decision by a higher court).

SETOFF A defendant's claim against the plaintiff, not connected with the original cause of action, used to reduce the plaintiff's recovery.

SETTLE 1. To reach an agreement, especially regarding a dispute that has not yet been taken to court. 2. To finish, or end, something. 3. To set up a trust. 4. To take up residence.

SETTLER A person who takes up residence, especially in the wilderness.

SETTLOR A person who establishes a trust.

SEVER To cut off; to separate.

SEVERABLE STATUTE A law that remains valid even though parts of it have been declared invalid by a court.

SEVERALTY OWNERSHIP Ownership entirely by one person.

SEVERANCE 1. Separation. 2. The destruction of a joint tenancy.

SHAM Phony; fake.

SHERMAN ANTITRUST ACT The first federal law passed to break up monopolies.

SHIRE-REEVE An old word for sheriff.

SHYSTER A crooked, dishonest lawyer, especially one who cheats his clients.

Sic Thus.

SIGNATURE The name of a person, written in that person's own hand.

SILENT PARTNER A business partner who does not appear to be a partner or whose name is not connected with the business, yet who invests in it and receives a share of the profits.

Simplex commendatio non obligat "A mere recommendation is not a warranty"; a thing that is recommended is not thus guaranteed to work.

SIMULATE To pretend to be.

SIMULATED Imitated; copied.

SINGLE PROPRIETORSHIP A business owned entirely by one person.

SKILLED WITNESS A witness who is educated or trained in a particular subject and is allowed to testify in court because of his expertise.

SLANDER The act of orally defaming a person with false and malicious spoken words.

SLANDER OF TITLE The act of making false and malicious statements about a plaintiff's title to property.

SLEEPING PARTNER A silent partner; a business partner who doesn't take an active part in running the business and whose name doesn't appear in the name of the business, yet who receives his share of the profits.

SLIP DECISION A ruling by the highest court of the county, or of a state, which is printed on a slip of paper and quickly distributed.

SMALL BUSINESS ADMINISTRATION (SBA) A federal agency providing advice, loans, and help for small businesses.

SMALL CLAIMS COURT A court that handles cases in which small sums of money are sought for alleged damages, often without the aid of lawyers.

SMART MONEY Money awarded to a plaintiff by a court in order to punish the defendant, in addition to money awarded for damages.

SMITH ACT A federal law requiring aliens to be fingerprinted and registered.

SMUGGLER A person who sneaks illegal goods, or goods that would otherwise be taxed, into a country.

SMUGGLING Secretly transporting into a country items that are illegal or would otherwise be taxed.

SMUT Obscene material.

SOCIAL SECURITY ADMINISTRATION A federal agency responsible for a government-run old-age and disability insurance program.

SODOMITE A person guilty of SODOMY.

SODOMY Unnatural sexual intercourse.

Solatium Damages that are awarded by a court for the plaintiff's wounded feelings.

SOLDIERS AND SAILORS CIVIL RELIEF ACT A federal law establishing special procedures for bringing civil suits against military personnel.

SOLE PROPRIETOR A person who owns an unincorporated business.

SOLE PROPRIETORSHIP An unincorporated business under the ownership of a single person.

SOLICITATION The act of enticing another to commit a crime.

SOLICITOR An attorney.

SOLICITOR GENERAL A federal attorney second in rank to the Attorney General. The Solicitor General represents the federal government in all civil cases involving the United States and assists the Attorney General whenever necessary.

SOLVENCY The ability of a person or a company to pay its debts.

SOLVENT A person or company able to pay its debts.

Son assault demesne A plea of self-defense against an assault charge.

SOVEREIGN IMMUNITY A government's immunity from being held liable in a lawsuit. This doesn't always bar suits against the government, however.

SPECIAL AGENT A representative of an employer, authorized to act on his employer's behalf in one specific matter.

SPECIAL TAIL An estate limited to the children of two people.

SPECIAL PROPERTY A property right that differs from ownership by entitling a person to obtain or retain possession of property only for a particular time or purpose.

SPECIALTY A contract bearing a seal.

SPECIFIC Precisely described.

SPECIFIC DENIAL A court's refusal to pursue a particular allegation in a complaint.

SPECIFIC PERFORMANCE 1. Performance of a contract precisely in the manner prescribed in the contract. 2. A remedy, sought by one party against the breaching party to a contract, that seeks precise compliance with the terms of the contract, rather than monetary damages.

SPEEDY TRIAL A constitutional right afforded to those charged with a crime allowing them to have their cases quickly brought to trial.

SPENDTHRIFT TRUST A trust set up to manage the estate of a person who is given to squandering his money. This prevents creditors from reaching the funds in trust.

SPITE FENCE A fence built for the purpose of angering or annoying a neighbor.

SPOLIATION The destruction, usually of some legal writing, done by someone unconnected with the writing.

Spoliatus debet ante omnia restitui "A robbery victim should first of all get back what was stolen."

STAKEHOLDER A person who holds the bets while the results of a wager are being awaited.

STALE CHECK A check that has been held for an excessive length of time before any attempt is made to cash it. Many states have laws limiting the length of time a check may be kept.

STALE DEMAND A claim or dispute that happened such a long time ago that it will not be allowed to be brought into court.

STAMP TAX A tax on items, such as cigarettes, that are marked with a stamp to show that the tax has been paid.

STAND The place in a courtroom where the witnesses sit or stand when giving testimony.

STAND AND DELIVER A traditional phrase used by highwaymen, meaning halt and hand over all your money.

STAND TRIAL, THE RIGHT TO The right of a defendant in a criminal action to have a court hear his case.

STANDARD OF CARE That standard to which a reasonable person would be held in order to avoid liability for negligent acts.

STANDING MUTE A defendant's refusal to plead guilty or not guilty in a criminal trial.

STANDING TO SUE A doctrine requiring a private citizen who complains in court of an unlawful act attributed to a government officer to prove that the acts invaded a legally protected interest of the plaintiff.

Stare decisis Let the decision stand; a court's policy of abiding by a decision established in the past.

Stare decisis et non quieta movere "Stand by established court decisions, and don't undermine preceding cases."

STATE SECRET Information that should not be revealed in a court of law, because its knowledge would endanger the country.

STATE'S EVIDENCE Testimony given by a criminal against other criminals, usually given in exchange for immunity from prosecution.

STATUS The relationship between an individual and the rest of the community.

STATUTE A law resulting from a legislative act.

STATUTE OF FRAUDS Legislation aimed at fraud arising out of verbal contracts. It requires that certain kinds of contracts be made in writing in order to be enforcible.

STATUTE OF LIMITATIONS Legislative acts that limit the amount of time a claimant has for bringing a suit against another person.

STATUTES OF WILLS State laws requiring that a will be properly written, signed, and witnessed in order to be valid.

STATUTES AT LARGE A collection of all the laws passed by a legislature in the order in which they were established.

STATUTORY That which is created, defined, or required by a statute.

STATUTORY LIENS Liens that arise out of some legislative act.

STATUTORY RAPE Unlawful sexual relations with a minor, with or without the minor's consent.

STAY 1. (v.) To postpone or stop, especially a legal proceeding. 2. (n.) A postponement (of something).

STAY OF EXECUTION The postponement of execution on a judgment; in other words, the postponement of the enforcement of a judgment, especially against a debtor.

STEAL To take and carry away another person's property without the right to do so.

STERILITY The lack of fertility; inability to produce offspring.

STIPENDIARY ESTATE An estate left to a person in return for his services.

STIPULATION An important part of an agreement, which has been demanded by one of the parties to the agreement.

STOCK 1. The capital with which a merchant operates. 2. Goods on hand. 3. Shares of ownership in a corporation.

STOCK DIVIDEND Corporate profits that are passed on to stockholders in the form of additional shares of stock.

STOCKHOLDER'S DERIVATIVE SUIT A suit in which a stockholder sues in his name for a right that belongs to a corporation.

STOLEN A condition of property that is no longer under the control of its lawful owner, due to theft.

STOP ORDER A notice sent by a depositor to his bank, telling the bank to stop payment on a check the depositor has written.

STOPPAGE *in transitu* The right of an unpaid seller to stop delivery of goods being delivered to a buyer by a carrier.

STRAW MAN 1. A person whose name is used as a "front" for promoting a business deal. 2. A person whose profession is to give false testimony in court.

STRICT LIABILITY The liability for some injury or damage even if the party held liable was not at fault or negligent.

Strictissimi juris The strictest application of the law.

STRIKE 1. (n.) A work stoppage by employees for the purpose of getting higher wages or benefits from an employer. 2. (v.) To remove, erase, or take out.

Sua sponte Voluntarily; of his own will.

SUBDIVIDE In real estate, to break up a piece of land into smaller lots (subdivisions), usually for the purpose of building single-family dwellings.

Sub nomine Under the name (of).

SUBLET To rent out something (e.g., an apartment) that is already being rented from someone else. A tenant sublets an apartment that he rents from the landlord.

SUBORNATION OF PERJURY The crime of causing a witness to lie under oath.

Subpoena A court order requiring a person to appear and testify at a trial or hearing.

Subpoena duces tecum A court order requiring a person to bring specified documents to the court.

SUBROGATION The transfer to another person of the creditor's right to claim a lawful debt.

SUBSCRIBE 1. To sign one's name at the end of a document. 2. To agree to buy stock in a company.

SUBSECTION A part of a section in a contract, statute, or book.

SUBSIDIARY Under the control of another, especially a company that is owned and controlled by another, larger company.

SUBSTANTIAL DAMAGES Considerable compensation for a genuine injury; as opposed to nominal damages.

SUBSTANTIAL PERFORMANCE The performance of a contract to the extent that the purpose of the contract is accomplished even though minor details are omitted.

SUBSTANTIVE LAW The law of rights and duties, rather than of procedure to enforce those rights.

SUBSTITUTED SERVICE Service of process in ways, authorized by statute, other than directly to the defendant in person.

SUBSURFACE RIGHTS Rights to what is found underneath a piece of land.

SUCCESSION Transfer of title to property under the laws of descent.

SUDDEN PASSION Immediate and intense emotions of hatred, rage, jealousy, etc., that result in an immediate homicide.

SUE To begin or continue a civil lawsuit.

SUFFRAGE The right to vote in political elections.

Sui generis One of a kind.

Sui juris A person who possesses the ability to make a contract.

SUICIDE 1. The crime of taking one's own life. 2. A person who takes his own life.

SUIT An action in a civil court.

SUMMARY Abbreviated; (something that is) done quickly.

SUMMARY JUDGMENT A judgment made before the conclusion of a trial because the outcome is clear.

SUMMARY PROCEEDINGS Shortcuts allowed by law to do away with court delays. Often used to dispossess tenants for nonpayment of rent.

SUMMONS A writ informing a person that he has been named as a defendant in a lawsuit and stating the time he is expected to appear in court.

SUPERSEDE To replace such as when an old law is replaced with a newer law or when a corporate officer is replaced by a person newly appointed to the post.

Supersedeas A judge's order to temporarily halt the legal proceedings in another court.

SUPERSEDING CAUSE An outside act or force coming between the negligent act of a person and the potential injury to another, thus preventing the actor from being held liable. For example, if a pedestrian is saved from being run over by a reckless driver because of a stop sign in the way of the driver, the stop sign is considered a superseding cause.

SUPERVENING CAUSE Negligence that later causes injury to a plaintiff.

SUPPLEMENTARY PROCEEDINGS Proceedings to determine which property owned by a debtor can be used to satisfy the demands of a creditor.

SUPPRESS EVIDENCE To willfully keep information from a jury, especially illegally gotten evidence.

Suppressio veri, expressio falsi "Suppress the truth, express falseness"; suppressing the truth is equal to telling a lie.

SUPPRESSION The hiding of facts, especially from a jury.

Supra Above.

SURCHARGE An excess amount of money charged for goods or services.

SURETY A person who agrees to be responsible for the obligations of another should those obligations not be met.

SURPLUS Extra.

SURPLUSAGE Something that is unnecessary or surplus; a matter that is needlessly brought to the attention of the court.

SURRENDER 1. To give up. 2. To return something, especially a right.

SURROGATE 1. A substitution for something. 2. In some states, a title given to a judge in a probate court.

SURTAX A tax on something that has already been taxed.

SURVEY 1. To determine the boundaries of a piece of land. 2. To examine something.

SURVIVOR A living relative of a decedent.

SURVIVORSHIP A right to property owned by a group, family, or partnership when all but one of the members dies.

SUSPEND To postpone something with the intent of later resuming it.

SUSPENDED SENTENCE A sentence that a judge decides either to postpone or to withhold because of the defendant's previously clean record as an incentive to future good conduct on the part of the defendant or for a variety of other reasons.

SUSPENSION The temporary removal of someone from some position, office, or duty.

SUSPICION A belief not based on proof.

SUSTAIN To support, approve, or permit something; often, a judge's approval of an objection voiced by an attorney in the courtroom.

SWEATSHOP A factory in which workers are underpaid and overworked.

SYNDICATE A group of people formed for the purpose of undertaking some enterprise too large for an individual.

SYLLABUS An abstract or summary, at the beginning of a case history, that outlines the important issues brought up in the case.

T

TACIT Inferred or understood.

TAFT-HARTLEY ACT A federal law regulating labor disputes.

TAIL 1. (v.) To limit, curtail, or reduce. 2. (n.) An estate limited to the decedent's children, grandchildren, and so forth.

TAKE 1. (v.) To carry away; to acquire. 2. (n.) Profits.

Tales de circumstantibus Jurors selected from onlookers.

TALESMEN Jurors selected to fill vacancies in a regular jury.

TALMUD A book containing the civil and religious laws of the Jewish people.

TAMPER To alter; to unlawfully meddle or interfere (with something), especially a jury or a legal document.

TANGIBLE Having form and substance.

TARIFF 1. A tax, especially on imported goods. 2. A schedule or list of prices.

TAX Money that is collected from a person in order to support government programs.

TAX *ad valorem* A tax based on the value of the item subject to tax.

TAX APPORTIONMENT The determining of who gets taxed for what.

TAX EVASION Avoiding full payment of a tax, especially income tax.

TAX SALE The selling of land at auction for the purpose of paying taxes.

TAXATION The process a government uses to raise revenue or to control something, by exacting payment from people or property.

TELLER 1. A person whose job is to keep a tally. Example: a

person who counts votes. 2. An employee of a bank who pays out and receives money from depositors.

TEMPORARY RESTRAINING ORDER (T.R.O.) A court's order stopping the activities of one party, which otherwise might cause irreparable damage, until a hearing can be held.

TENANCY 1. Real property leased by a tenant. 2. The status of a person who leases or has a right to possess real property belonging to another.

TENANCY BY THE ENTIRETY Joint ownership of property by a husband and wife. At the death of one, the other becomes the sole owner.

TENANCY IN COMMON The holding of real property or personalty by various persons under two or more titles. Each party can dispose of his interest as he chooses.

TENANT A person who has possession of real property belonging to a landlord.

TENANT AT WILL One holding possession of real property by permission of the owner, and not for a fixed term.

TENANT FOR LIFE A person who has a right to a piece of real property during his lifetime or for the lifetime of others.

TENDER An offer of money or of some other property in order to fulfill an obligation.

TENEMENT 1. Anything of a permanent nature that can be owned. 2. An apartment building.

TENOR The true intent or purpose of a legal document when contrary to the actual wording.

TENURE A manner of holding lands or positions, as dictated by someone in charge of the matter, usually with regard to time.

TERM 1. A word or phrase. 2. A condition to the performance of contract. 3. A fixed period of time.

TERMINABLE INTEREST An interest in property that will end at a certain time or at the occurrence of some event.

TERMINATE To end, or cease.

TERMINATION OF CONTRACT The end of contractual obligations and benefits by the parties to the contract.

TERMINATION OF OFFER The withdrawal of an offer.

TERRITORIAL WATERS A part of the ocean off the coast of a country that is recognized as being within the national boundaries of that country.

TERRITORY 1. A geographic part of a nation that is not yet incorporated as a state, province, or district. 2. A geographical area where a court has jurisdiction. 3. An area where a salesman operates.

TESTACY The leaving of a valid will.

TESTAMENT A will or disposition of real and personal property of a decedent.

TESTAMENTARY Having something to do with a will or resulting from a will.

Testamentum omne morte consummatur "A will can be perfected only after the death of the person who left it."

TESTATOR 1. Someone who makes or has made a will. 2. A decedent who leaves a will.

TESTATRIX A woman who leaves a will.

Testes ponderantur, non numerantur "Witnesses are weighed, not numbered."

TESTIMONY Statements made by a competent witness under oath.

THEFT An act of larceny.

THIEF Someone who takes property of others without their consent, with the intent to use it for himself.

THIRD DEGREE A broad term for illegal acts performed by the police in order to extract confessions from persons accused of committing crimes.

THIRD-PARTY BENEFICIARY A person who can maintain an action for the enforcement of a contract made between two other parties and intended for his benefit.

THREAT An intent, to cause harm to another, that is communicated to that person.

THREE-MILE LIMIT Formerly, a nation's border extended three miles from shore, which was the distance a cannonball could be fired.

TICKET 1. A piece of paper that entitles the holder to some privilege described on the paper. 2. A citation issued by an authorized officer for some violation of the law.

TIPSTAFF A term referring to a police officer assigned to keep the peace inside the courtroom, serve summonses, and guard prisoners. The term comes from medieval England, where such officers were armed with a staff having an ornate metal tip that served as both a weapon and a badge of authority.

TITLE A valid right to possess ownership of something.

TITLE COMPANY A company that investigates the title to property that is being sold in order to ensure that the seller of the property actually holds the title.

TITLE SEARCH The act of investigating a title in order to prove ownership and to discover any covenants binding upon a piece of real property.

TO LET To make something available for rent.

TO WIT That is to say; I mean.

TONTINE A partnership of several members who make annual payments into a fund that will be claimed by the longest-living partner.

TORT A private or civil wrongdoing, usually resulting from a breach of some duty that is due an injured party. Libel, assault, and negligence are examples of tort.

TORT CLAIMS ACT A federal statute establishing procedure for bringing tort claims against the United States Government.

TORT LAW The area of the law dealing with civil wrongs.

TORTFEASOR A person who commits a private or civil wrong.

TORTIOUS A term that describes an act that results in a tort.

TORTURE The causing of bodily pain either to punish, or to obtain information from, another person.

TOTAL LOSS The complete destruction of an insured piece of property, especially automobiles or buildings, which would make restoration or repair of the damaged property uneconomical for the insurance company.

Totidem verbis In so many words.

TOTTEN TRUST A bank account in the name of the depositor as trustee for another, so if the depositor should die, the entire amount in the bank becomes the property of the survivor. This type of trust can be ended by the depositor at any time.

TOWNSHIP 1. A surveyed parcel of public land six miles square. 2. A small town.

TRADE NAME The name by which a company does its business, so that the public will know with whom it is doing business.

TRADE USAGE The language and customs commonly used among those engaged in particular trades.

TRADEMARK A distinctive design, affixed to a product or to the product's container, by which it can be recognized as the product of a particular producer.

TRADER A person in the business of buying and selling merchandise.

TRAFFIC 1. The sale and exchange of commercial goods, both legal and illegal. 2. The coming and going of motor vehicles upon a road.

TRAFFIC ACCIDENT A mishap, involving one or more forms of transportation (automobiles, trucks, pedestrians), that takes place on a public road.

TRANSACTION A business deal.

TRANSCRIPT A copy of something written or spoken.

TRANSFER To convey or pass title to property from one person to another.

TRANSFERRED INTENT Meaning to do harm to a person but accidentally doing harm to another instead.

TRANSITORY ACTION A court action that may be undertaken

in any geographical jurisdiction the defendant might be in; a court action that is not required to take place in the county or state where the cause of action arose or the subject matter is.

TREASON "Treason in the United States shall consist . . . in the levying of war against them"—United States Constitution; generally, rendering aid to the enemy.

TREASURE Hidden valuables of unknown ownership.

TRESPASS 1. (v.) To do injury (to another person) or to damage (property belonging to someone) by doing an unlawful act or by acting in an unlawful manner. 2. (n.) An entry, without permission, on another's property.

TRESPASS *de bonis asportatis* A form of trespass in which goods or personal property is carried away by the trespasser.

TRESPASS *quare clausum fregit* Unlawful passing upon another's land.

TRESPASSER A person who does injury to another person or property by doing an unlawful act or by acting in an unlawful manner.

TRESPASSER *ab initio* In some states, a person who lawfully enters onto another's property and commits a crime, thereby making the entry unlawful.

TRIAL An examination by a judicial court of the issues presented by the parties to a civil or criminal lawsuit within the court's jurisdiction.

TRIBUNAL 1. A court, especially a court with more than one judge. 2. A place where cases are heard.

TROVER An action to recover property lost by the plaintiff and found, but not returned, by the defendant.

TRUE BILL An indictment that has been endorsed by a grand jury after having heard the evidence and having been satisfied of the truth of the accusation.

TRUST A right in property held by a trustee for a beneficiary. The trustee must deal with the property with great care and faithfulness to the beneficiary.

TRUST BENEFICIARY A person who receives a benefit from a trust.

TRUST FUND Money held in trust.

TRUST RECEIPT The title to goods that the seller gives to the person lending money so the buyer can purchase the goods. The lender holds the title until the buyer pays off the loan.

TRUSTEE Someone who is empowered to hold property for the benefit of another. Legal title rests with the trustee, but he can use the property only for the other's benefit, not his own.

TRUSTOR One who creates a trust.

TRUTH-IN-LENDING ACT A piece of legislation that demands that a prospective borrower be aware of the finance charges he will incur.

Turpis causa Immoral consideration, which a court will not recognize. For example, if a man pays another to murder his wife and no murder takes place, the husband cannot sue the hired murderer for breaking a contract.

TURPITUDE Dishonest, immoral, or unjust activity.

TWELVE-MILE LIMIT An off-shore boundary, twelve miles from land, established by an agreement between the United States and Great Britain during Prohibition, allowing the search of British ships within the twelve-mile limit for illegal liquor.

TWO-HUNDRED-MILE LIMIT Today, United States boundaries extend two hundred miles from shore.

TYING IN The practice of refusing to sell a product unless another product is also bought. For example, a storekeeper might want to stock Brand X paint, but he cannot buy Brand X paint unless he also buys Brand X paint thinner.

◀ U ▶

ULTIMATUM A final offer or demand.

Ultra vires A term for an illegal act performed by a corporation, or any act beyond the scope of powers granted in the corporation's charter.

UN The abbreviation for the United Nations.

Una voce Literally, with one voice; a unanimous decision.

UNARMED 1. Defenseless. 2. Having no weapons.

UNCONSCIONABILITY A term for some act or agreement that is outrageous and offensive to a person's sensibilities, because of its being one-sided or otherwise unfair.

UNCONSTITUTIONAL A term for something in violation of the liberties guaranteed by the Constitution.

UNCONTESTED DIVORCE A divorce action that is not challenged by either party.

UNDERTAKING 1. An enforcible promise, made by one party during a legal proceeding, as opposed to mutual promises made in a contract. 2. A venture or enterprise.

UNDERWRITE To insure. To underwrite something means to guarantee that it will be paid for.

UNDERWRITER A person or company that insures another.

UNDUE INFLUENCE Persuasion of such a nature that it overpowers the free will of a person, causing him to act contrary to his own free will. Often used in regard to pressures put on a person making a will.

UNETHICAL CONDUCT Behavior that is not in keeping with professional standards.

UNFAIR BARGAIN A situation in which one party unreasonably takes advantage of another.

UNFAIR COMPETITION A broad term descriptive of fraudulent and deceitful rivalry between businesses. Often used when one company tries to supplant another in the marketplace not by competing but by imitating the competitor to mislead the public.

UNFAIR LABOR PRACTICE A statutory term for an employer's acts that seek to hinder labor organizing.

UNIFORM COMMERCIAL CODE A set of laws to which merchants are subject and that differ very little from state to state.

UNILATERAL One-sided.

UNION SHOP A business that employs only union members.

UNITED STATES CODE ANNOTATED (U.S.C.A.) A compilation of federal laws that are codified and described.

UNITED STATES CODE OF MILITARY JUSTICE (U.S.C.M.J.) A collection of laws that govern the military personnel of the United States.

UNITED STATES COURT OF APPEALS (U.S.C.A.) Federal courts that hear appeals from the federal district courts.

UNJUST ENRICHMENT A doctrine that provides for restitution when one party unfairly procures something of value at the expense of another party or retains something that should belong to another.

UNLAWFUL That which is against the law.

UNLAWFUL ASSEMBLY A common-law crime consisting of three or more persons disturbing the public peace and intending to perform some violent and unlawful act, but before acts to that end are taken.

UNLAWFUL DETAINER Retaining possession of the land of another, after one's right to hold it has ended. Example: a tenant who does not leave at the end of his lease when asked to do so.

UNLIQUIDATED ASSETS Generally meaning unsold assets, so that a definite value cannot be set.

Uno flatu Literally, with one breath; in one movement.

UNWRITTEN LAW 1. Specifically, a rule that killing a spouse's lover is not against the law. This is not recognized by the courts. 2. A law that is the result of the customs of a particular place and that has not been enacted as a statute or ordinance.

URBAN Belonging to a city or town.

USAGE A custom or practice followed by a trade, especially the language or terms unique to a particular trade, which the parties to a contract are presumed to be aware of.

USE The enjoyment (of something) that belongs to someone else.

USUFRUCT A right to use and profit from property belonging to another so long as that property is not changed or damaged.

USURY Interest rates in excess of those set by law.

UTTER 1. To present or offer as genuine something that is a forgery. 2. To make public or put forth.

Uxor (*Ux.*) Wife.

UXORICIDE The killing of a wife by her husband.

V

V. An abbreviation for *versus* (against), commonly used in the names of court cases, such as *Hadley* v. *Baxendale.*

V.A. The abbreviation for the Veterans Administration.

VACANT Unoccupied, empty.

VACATE To annul, or set aside.

VAGRANCY A minor offense consisting of loitering, idleness, or having no visible means of support.

VAGUE Uncertain and indefinite.

VALID Legally binding. Authentic.

VENDEE A person who buys something; a buyer.

VENDOR Someone who sells something; a seller.

Venire facias An order given to a sheriff to summon a jury.

VENUE 1. The location where a wrong has been committed. 2. The county where a case is to be tried.

VERDICT The formal decision made by a jury concerning the matters brought before it in the course of a trial.

VESTED Absolute; established; giving absolute ownership.

VESTED INTEREST Ownership or interest in a piece of property that is under physical possession or will be in the future. For example, if a person inherits a house, that person has a vested interest in the house even before he can move in.

VEXATION A harassment, irritation, or annoyance.

Vi et armis "With force and arms."

Via antiqua via est tuta "The old ways are the safest."

VIABILITY An unborn child's ability to exist outside the womb.

VICARIOUS LIABILITY Liability imposed on one person for the

actions of another. Example: A parent may be liable for an accident his child causes in the family car.

VIDUITY The state of being a widow; widowhood.

VIGILANTE COMMITTEE An organized group attempting to create order in a lawless society.

Vigilantibus et non dormientibus jura subveniunt "Justice aids the vigilant, not those who sleep on their rights."

VIOLATION An act that is contrary to statutory law or administrative regulations.

VOID Hollow: without legal force; not binding.

VOIDABLE Describing that which does not obligate the parties or that can be made void but isn't void in itself.

Voir dire (Fr.) An examination of a person as a prospective juror, to test his competency and prejudices.

Volenti non fit injuria "He who gives his permission to be injured cannot sue the party injuring him."

VOLSTEAD ACT An act passed by Congress in 1919 and repealed in 1933, which prohibited the sale of liquor in the United States.

VOLUNTARY Not impelled; acting on one's own initiative without being paid to do so.

VOLUNTEER A person who acts without an express or implied promise of being paid.

VOTING TRUST An accumulation of shares in a corporation, belonging to several parties, that are voted as a block under certain guidelines.

VOUCHER Written proof of a transaction; a receipt.

Vs. An abbreviation for *versus*.

◀ W ▶

WAGE 1. (v.) To carry on, as in "wage war." 2. (n.) The amount earned by a worker over a specific period of time.

WAGER A bet or gamble.

WAIVER An oral or written statement voluntarily yielding or abandoning a legal right or claim. Conduct that shows an intention to waive a right is an implied waiver.

WANTON ACT A reckless deed, committed without regard for the rights or safety of others, akin to willful misconduct.

WARD 1. A person, usually a minor or mental incompetent, under the care of a guardian. 2. A district or neighborhood within a city.

WARDEN A title meaning the same as guardian or keeper. For example, a game warden's job is to guard game animals from poachers.

WARD OF THE COURT A person, usually a minor or a mental incompetent, under the care of the court.

WAREHOUSEMAN A person in business to accept and store goods in his warehouse for profit.

WAREHOUSE RECEIPT A receipt given by a warehouseman to a party whose goods are being stored in the warehouse.

WARRANT 1. (v.) To make a promise. 2. (n.) A written order issued by a court or other competent authority authorizing the actions of an officer.

WARRANT OF ARREST A written order issued by a court authorizing the seizure and detainment of a person.

WARRANTY A guarantee.

WARRANTY OF FITNESS A guarantee by a seller that goods sold are suitable for the buyer's special purpose.

WARRANTY OF MERCHANTABILITY A guarantee by a seller that goods sold are fit for the general uses of the goods.

WATCH AND WARD The watch is the night shift in a police station; the ward is the day shift.

WATCHMAN A private guard whose job is to watch over and protect property entrusted to his care.

WATERCOURSE A brook, stream, creek, river, or canal.

WATERED STOCK Stock that is issued by a company but not fully paid for.

WEAPON Any object that is used, or intended for use, as a tool for fighting or for causing injury.

WEIGHT OF EVIDENCE The believability of evidence brought into court.

WERGILD A fine for killing someone, in Anglo-Saxon England.

WHARFAGE Money paid for the use of a wharf to load or unload cargo onto or from ships.

WHARFINGER A person who owns or manages a wharf, or dock, from which cargo is loaded onto or unloaded from ships.

WHEREBY By which, in accordance with which.

WHEREFORE 1. Why. 2. Because.

WHIPLASH An injury resulting from the victim's head being whipped or snapped forward, backward, or to the side, usually in an auto accident.

WHIPPING POST A pole or stake to which a prisoner is tied in order to be whipped as a punishment.

WHITE LIGHTNING Illegally manufactured corn whiskey.

WHITE SLAVERY The transportation of females across state lines for immoral purposes, usually prostitution.

WHOLESALE PRICE The price of goods charged to a storekeeper, or retailer, by a wholesaler.

WIFE A married woman.

WILDCAT STRIKE A strike by union workers that is unauthorized by the union officials.

WILL 1. A desire, wish, or inclination. 2. A legal expression, usually written, of a person's wishes regarding the disposal of his property after his death. It is revocable while its maker is alive.

WILLFUL Intentional and voluntary; literally, full of will.

WILLFUL AND WANTON Intentionally and recklessly unmindful of the rights of others.

WINDFALL An unforeseen profit or gain.

WIRETAPPING Listening to conversations made on the telephone without the knowledge or permission of the parties involved in the conversation.

WISHES OF THE CHILD An element considered by the court in deciding which party in a divorce should get custody of the child.

WITHDRAWAL 1. The removal of money from a bank. 2. The abandonment of a crime by a member of a gang.

WITNESS 1. A spectator. 2. Someone who can attest to the authenticity of a document. 3. Someone who testifies in court, under oath, about what he knows.

WOOD LEAVE A license to cut and remove timber on a specified tract of land.

WORKMEN'S COMPENSATION ACTS Legislative acts designed to compensate an employee or his dependents for his injury or death suffered during the course of employment, whether or not negligence was an issue.

WOUND An injury to the body as a result of an act of violence.

WRIT A written command of the court issued to an officer, directing him to act in some way.

WRIT OF ATTACHMENT A court's order to the sheriff to force a person to appear before the judge and explain why the judgment of the court has not been obeyed.

WRIT OF EXECUTION A court's order to put in force the judgment of the court.

WRONG A violation of the legal rights of another; an injury to person or property.

WRONGFUL-DEATH STATUTE A statute that allows a survivor or the executor of a decedent's estate the right to sue for any wrongful act or negligence that caused the death of the decedent.

◀ X ▶

X 1. A mark representing the signature of a person who cannot write. 2. A symbol used to represent an unknown thing.

◀ Y ▶

YELLOW-DOG CONTRACT A contract that requires an employee to refrain from becoming a member of a labor union under pain of dismissal.

YIELD 1. (v.) To surrender, or give up, something. 2. (v.) To comply with something that is demanded. 3. (n.) A return on an investment of money or of labor.

◂ Z ▸

ZONING The practice of dividing the property contained within a city or county into districts or zones for the purpose of regulating the use or size of the buildings and plots within the districts.

Appendix A

COMMON-LAW CRIMES

The common law originated in England many centuries ago and greatly influenced the modern laws of the United States, although the two are not identical. This Appendix is presented to give the reader a historical sketch of the laws from which our own statutes have descended.

CRIMES AGAINST THE KING, GOVERNMENT OR COURTS

Barratry
Bribery
Champerty
Compounding crime (see COMPOUNDING A FELONY)
Conspiracy
Contempt
Counterfeiting
Embracery
Escape
Maintenance
Misconduct of office
Misprision of felony
Obstruction of justice
Perjury and subornation
Piracy

CRIMES AGAINST MORALITY

Adultery
Bigamy
Blasphemy
Fornication
Illicit cohabitation
Incest
Mistreatment of corpses
Obscenity and indecency
Prostitution
Seduction
Sodomy

CRIMES AGAINST THE PUBLIC PEACE

Carrying weapons
Fighting
Forcible entry and detainer
Keeping a disorderly house
Libel
Riot
Unlawful assembly
Vagrancy

CRIMES AGAINST THE PERSON

Abduction
Abortion
Assault
Battery
Blackmail
Contraceptivism
Dueling
Extortion
False imprisonment
Involuntary manslaughter
Manslaughter
Murder
Rape
Robbery

CRIMES AGAINST HABITATION

Arson
Burglary

CRIMES AGAINST PROPERTY

Blackmail
Concealing stolen property
Counterfeiting
Embezzlement
Extortion
Forgery
Larceny
Presentation of false pretenses
Receiving stolen property
Robbery
Theft
Uttering

Appendix B

LATIN PREFIXES

PREFIX	MEANING	EXAMPLE
a, ab, abs	away from, from, out, up	absence, abscond
ac, ad, af, al, an, ap, as, at	to	accelerate, advance, affect, alert, analyze, appeal, aspire, attain
am, amb, ambi	about, around, both	ambiguous, ambidextrous
bi	twice, two	biplane
co, col, com, con, cor	with, joint, together	coexist, collect, community, conduct, corroborate
contra	against, opposite, prohibit	contravention
de	down, separate	decline
dis	apart, deprive, separate	dismember
e, ef, ex	from, off, out of	educe, effect, export
em, en	in, into	employ, entrust
i, il, im, in, ir	not	ignorant, illegitimate, imperfect, insolvent, irresponsible

PREFIX	MEANING	EXAMPLE
inter, intro	between, within	intercollegiate, introduce
ir	in, into	irradiate
mal, male	bad, evil, ill	malady, malevolent
non	not	nonchalant
ob, op	against, in the way of, opposed to	obstruct, opposition
par	part	participate
per	by means of, through	performance
post	after, following	postpone
pre	before	precede
preter	beyond, past	pretermission
pro	before, for, forward, in behalf of	proceed
quasi	as if, not entirely	quasi contract
re	again, back, backward	retard
retro	backward, reverse	retrospect
se, sed	apart, aside	section, sediment
semi	half, partially	semifinalist
sub, suc, suf, sus	below, under	submarine, succumb, suffocate, suspend
super, supra	above, over	superpower, supernatural
trans	across, beyond, over, through	transparent
ultra	beyond, excessive, extreme	ultramodern
un, uni	one	unite, universe
vice	in place of	vice-president

LATIN SUFFIXES

SUFFIX	MEANING	EXAMPLE
age	condition	tutelage
al	like, suitable for	instrumental
ant	actor, agent, doer	defendant
ary	belonging to, relating to	auxiliary
ate	function or office	protectorate
cle, cule	diminutive	particle, molecule
ess	feminine	hostess
ette	diminutive	cigarette
ice	act, condition	accomplice
ise, ize	application of action denoted by a verb	expertise, specialize
ine	in the nature of	marine
ion	denotes a state of being	dominion
ment	act, instrument	endorsement
mony	instrument, means of	alimony
on	augment, increase	automaton
ory	location, place	observatory
sion, tion	denotes a state of being	tension, condition
tude	denotes noun derived from an adjective	attitude
ty	condition, quality, state	guaranty
ure	action or result	tenure

GREEK PREFIXES

PREFIX	MEANING	EXAMPLE
a, an	not, without	amoral
amphi	on both sides	amphitheater

PREFIX	MEANING	EXAMPLE
ana	according to, again, back, up	analogy
anti	against, opposite	antitank
apo, aph	away from, from	apogee, aphasia
arch	chief, main	archangel
auto	self	automobile
cat, cata	away, back, down	catacomb, catapult
di	twice, two	diagonal
dia	apart, through	dialysis
dys	bad, difficult, ill	dysentery
e, ec, ex	out of	elation, eccentric, excrete
em, en	in	emboss, endanger
endo	inner	endoskeleton
ep, epi	upon	epidermal
eu	well	eulogy, euphoric
hemi	half	hemisphere
hyp, hypo	under	hypnotic, hypodermic
hyper	above, over	hypercritical
met	after, over	metaphor
mon, mono	alone, one	monorail
ortho	right	orthopedic
pan	all	pandemic
par, para	beside	parameter
peri	around, round	perimeter
pro	before	procreation
pros	toward	prospect
proto	first	prototype
syl, syn	along with, with	syllabus, syndicate

GREEK SUFFIXES

SUFFIX	MEANING	EXAMPLE
ic	having to do with	Hellenic
ism	act, condition, state	optimism
ist	one who does or professes	optimist
sis	action, condition, state	analysis
sy	action, condition, state	heresy
y	an activity, quality	hasty